TOO SCARED TO CRY

Also by Maggie Hartley

Too Scared to Cry

AND OTHER TRUE STORIES FROM THE NATION'S FAVOURITE FOSTER CARER

MAGGIE HARTLEY

Too Scared to Cry first published in eBook only in Great Britain in 2016
A Family for Christmas first published in eBook only in Great Britain in 2016
The Girl No One Wanted first published in eBook only in Great Britain in 2017
This omnibus edition first published in 2018 by Trapeze,
an imprint of The Orion Publishing Group Ltd
Carmelite House, 50 Victoria Embankment,
London EC4Y 0DZ

An Hachette UK company

5 7 9 10 8 6 4

A CIP catalogue record for this book is
available from the British Library.

ISBN (Paperback): 978 1 4091 7981 8
ISBN (eBook): 978 1 4091 8031 9

Typeset by Born Group

Printed in Great Britain by CPI Group (UK) Ltd, Croydon CR0 4YY

www.orionbooks.co.uk

Dedication

This book is dedicated to Ben, Damien, Noah, Edward, Leanne and Louisa and all the children and teenagers who have passed through my home. It's been a privilege to have cared for you and to be able to share your stories. And to the children who live with me now. Thank you for your determination, strength and joy and for sharing your lives with me.

Contents

A Message from Maggie

I wanted to write this book to give people an honest account of what it's like to be a foster carer. To talk about some of the challenges that I face on a day-to-day basis and some of the children that I've helped.

My main concern throughout is to protect the children who have been in my care. For this reason, all names and identifying details have been changed, including my own, and no locations have been included. But I can assure you that all my stories are based on real-life cases and are told from my own experiences.

Being a foster carer is a privilege, and I couldn't imagine doing anything else. My house is never quiet, but I wouldn't have it any other way. I hope perhaps my stories will inspire other people to consider fostering, as new carers are always desperately needed.

Maggie Hartley

Too Scared to Cry

ONE

The Sound of Silence

It wasn't your normal Sunday night in our house. While most people were having a quiet evening in front of the telly, getting ready for their first day back at work or school after the weekend, we were having a showdown.

You see, my seventeen-year-old foster daughter Kate had just dropped the bombshell that she was pregnant.

'Oh Kate,' I sighed. 'Why?'

'After everything that's happened with my family, I just want a family of my own,' she told me.

'But we are your family,' I said.

'I know you are but it's not the same,' she said.

I understood what she meant because I'd seen it in teenagers who had grown up in the care system many times before. That desperate need to have someone who biologically belonged to them. A blood relative. A baby would love her unconditionally, whereas her own parents hadn't. It didn't mean I was happy about the news though.

'You know that you and the baby can live here,' I said.

'There's no question of that. I'm just a little bit disappointed that's all.'

Kate was halfway through a course in nursery nursing at the local college. She and her boyfriend Karl had a volatile relationship and they weren't together any more. I'd wanted her to finish her course and find a job, not be struggling to get by as a single mum. I had wanted her to get settled on her own and enjoy independence for a while first.

'Do you want to ring your social worker and tell her the news or shall I?' I asked.

'Please, Maggie, will you do it?' she said sheepishly. 'I don't think she's going to be very happy about it.'

'I think you're right,' I said.

Kate's social worker Marion wasn't one to mince words, and would be sure to tell her straight. Kate was seventeen and would be out of the care system in less than a year, on her own and with a child of her own to care for. Although there was nothing we could have done to stop her getting pregnant, I knew Marion would be as disappointed as I was.

I'd been fostering Kate for the past four years, ever since her relationship with her parents had broken down. Her father had thrown her out and Social Services had placed her with me. Since then, she'd slowly taken steps in the right direction. I couldn't help feeling that this was a bit of a setback.

'Why are you arguing?' asked eight-year-old Oliver, coming down the stairs.

'We're not arguing, lovey,' I said. 'Kate and I are having a discussion about something.'

Oliver had come to live with me around the same time as Kate. He'd been put into care by his mother who couldn't cope with his disruptive behaviour. With his big blue eyes and golden ringlets, he looked like butter wouldn't melt in his mouth. But he'd run rings round me to start with. He'd lashed out, had awful tantrums and used terrible language. I'd soon realised that it was about attention which he hadn't got much of at home and he'd soon settled down. No attempt to rehome him with his mum had worked, so he'd been with me ever since.

We were interrupted by the phone ringing.

'Let me just get this and we'll talk some more later,' I told Kate. 'And Ollie you need to get to bed.'

'It's OK,' she sighed. 'I'm tired. I'm going to go up to my room too.'

I could see she was upset that I was disappointed in her.

'Maggie?' said a voice as I picked up the phone. 'It's Clare, one of the duty social workers from Social Services.'

'Oh, hi Clare,' I said. 'What can I do for you?'

'We've got a bit of a situation with Pat and I wondered if you might be able to help.'

Pat was another single foster carer who lived in the same area as me.

'She's got a chest infection,' she told me. 'It's been hanging around for weeks but it's got worse and she's really poorly. She's on antibiotics and I think she just needs a week or so in bed to recover.'

'Poor Pat,' I said.

'That obviously means she can't look after the children she's got living with her at the minute,' continued Clare. 'So I wondered if you'd be willing to help out as respite and have them for a couple of weeks while Pat gets herself right?'

'Of course,' I said. 'I know Pat would do the same for me if it was the other way round.'

I only had Oliver and Kate living with me, and it had been a couple of weeks since my last foster child had left – a twelve-year-old girl called Ruth who had been reunited with her birth mother. So I had a spare bedroom with bunk beds and a single bed in it.

'Who's Pat fostering?' I asked. 'To be honest I didn't even know that she'd got any new children in.'

'They only arrived four days ago.' Clare explained that it was a three-year-old and a four-year-old boy.

'Damian is the younger and Ben is the older,' she said. 'I doubt they'll give you any trouble, Maggie. I've never seen such quiet, timid little ones. Pat says they've barely said a word.'

They'd arrived with nothing but she said that Pat had already got them kitted out with clothes and basics.

'Well it sounds as if there's hardly anything for me to do,' I told her.

'OK, I'll drop them round to you tomorrow morning,' said Clare. 'I don't know much about this case to be honest but I'll try and give you a bit of background on the kids then. Thanks again for helping out.'

'No problem,' I said.

Well the week ahead was certainly shaping up to be a bit different than I had expected. With a pregnant teen and two new children coming to live with me, I had a feeling I was going to have my hands full.

Monday morning was the usual flurry of activity as I saw the kids off to college and school.

When everyone had left, I got to work making sure all the breakfast pots were cleared away and things were neat and tidy before Clare arrived with the children. The spare bedroom was all ready for them.

As I walked down the stairs I saw a shadow at the front door through the glass.

'Hello Maggie,' said Clare, as I opened it. 'This is Damian and Ben, who I was telling you about.'

They were beautiful children and they looked well cared for. They were mixed race with gorgeous curly dark hair and huge brown eyes. They weren't scrawny and they were wearing shiny new shoes and smart jackets.

'It's lovely to meet you both,' I said, crouching down so I was on their level. 'I'm Maggie. I know my friend Pat's been looking after you for a few days, but she's poorly, so you've come to stay with me for a little while.'

Neither of them said a word. They just stared at me with big, blinking eyes. As Clare walked into the hallway, they cowered behind her legs.

'They're very timid and they haven't said a thing since I picked them up,' she said quietly to me.

'I'm not surprised, they're probably scared and in shock,' I told her.

A few days ago they'd been taken away from their parents and now they were on the move again. They were probably wondering where the heck they were this time.

'I've got some toys in the kitchen you might like to come and have a look at,' I said, holding out my hands to them but neither of them reached out.

They followed Clare and I like two obedient little puppies.

I'd put some toys out on the kitchen floor to try and help the children to relax and feel at home. They both stood there stiffly.

'There are lots of things for you to play with,' I said, sitting down on the floor to try and encourage them to join me. 'There's Duplo so you can build something, a few jigsaws and some cars.'

They sat down but didn't touch anything.

'Would you like a cuppa, Clare?' I asked.

'Oh yes please,' she said.

I got up and put the kettle on and got out some mugs. When I looked round at Damian and Ben they were both still sat there. Neither of them had moved a muscle or shown any interest in any of the toys.

'How about a cup of juice and a biscuit?' I asked them.

Neither of them responded. I looked at Clare.

'I'm sure they'd like that,' she nodded.

I got them a beaker of cordial each and a custard cream, and put them down next to them on the floor. Again, they didn't touch them.

Clare and I sat at the kitchen table with our tea so we'd be out of immediate earshot of the children.

'So what can you tell me?' I asked quietly.

She explained that a few days ago Ben had been at preschool when he'd complained that his arms were sore.

'When a staff member had a look under his top she found that his arms were covered in bruises.

'Lots of little marks that looked like they were made by adult fingers grabbing him too tightly.'

Poor little mite.

'When the nursery staff asked them about it he said he'd been naughty and Daddy had got cross.'

Since then Social Services had interviewed their parents, Rob and Tracy, and both children had been checked over at hospital and found to have suspicious bruising.

'We've spoken to the mum and dad, who are denying everything, but we decided the safest thing was to take both children into care until we make a decision about the parents.'

'Rob is Ben and Damian's stepdad,' she said. 'They've also got a six-month-old son together who's still at home.'

I was surprised.

'How come you haven't removed the baby as well?' I asked.

'Well, he was also examined but there was no bruising or any injuries. There's nothing to suggest that Dad has touched him.

'We're monitoring them constantly and health visitors are going in every day to talk to the mum. For now, while we try and answer a few questions about the other two, we've decided the baby can stay.'

I looked over at the children who were still sat there in silence.

'What are the main priorities with these two?' I asked.

'Well as you can see, they're very, very quiet,' she said.

'Quiet doesn't even cover it,' I said. 'Neither of them has said a single word.'

'At this point we don't know if that's a result of the trauma of the past few days, although Ben's preschool did say he generally wasn't very verbal,' said Clare. 'All I can suggest is lots of play, in the hope that that will help encourage them to communicate or at least make some noise. I'm sure they'll be fine once they settle in.'

I hoped she was right. I was used to children coming to me scared, bewildered and confused, but I'd never seen a pair so frozen and silent as these two. After nearly an hour, they were still sat there like two statues.

'I'd better be going now,' Clare said. 'We'll keep in touch.'

As Clare stood up from the table, I saw Ben's expression change and I could sense his panic. Clare must have noticed it too.

'You'll be OK,' she told him. 'Maggie will look after you.'

I saw Clare out and went back into the kitchen.

'Right then, shall we go and have a look at your bedroom?' I asked the children.

They didn't say anything but they obediently followed me up the stairs. They were very compliant – everything I asked they did immediately.

'This is where you're going to sleep while you stay with me,' I told them, showing them the spare room.

Most children who are taken into care don't tend to have much, in fact you're lucky if you get a black bin bag filled with a few dirty clothes. But because Damian and Ben had been with Pat before coming to me, both of them had a little suitcase full of new clothes that were all washed and nicely folded, as well as toothbrushes, flannels and a soft toy each.

'What lovely teddies,' I said. 'I'll put them on your beds and shall we get your pyjamas out and put them under your pillow?'

I carried on talking to them even though they weren't responding.

'Let's put all these nice new clothes away,' I said.

As I put their clothes into drawers, I made an inventory of what each of them had in their suitcase, just like I did with every child who came to stay with me. It was important to send them on with exactly what they'd come with, and if I had a note of it there wouldn't be any dispute.

The kids just stood there watching me with wide eyes.

'Now, Clare told me that you like to watch cartoons. Shall I put some on for you when we go downstairs while I start preparing the dinner for later?'

I got no response.

'Oliver will be home from school soon so you can meet him,' I said. 'He's another little boy who lives with me.'

Ben and Damian sat silently in front of the TV while I was in the kitchen peeling and chopping potatoes. Soon I heard the front door go. I knew it would be Oliver so I went to let him in.

'Come and meet Damian and Ben,' I said. 'They're going to be staying with us for a couple of weeks as their foster carer isn't very well.'

'How old are they?' he asked.

'Only three and four,' I said. 'And they're a little bit shy and quiet, so it would be nice if you could help them feel at home.'

As soon as Oliver walked in the room, the two of them shot up and cowered behind my legs. In a way I was pleased as at least they were showing some sort of reaction and it was better than vacant faces.

'It's OK,' said Oliver gently. 'I was really shy when I came to Maggie's house too. Do you want to come and play?'

Ben shook his head.

'Maybe they can sit and watch you,' I said.

Oliver, bless him, started to build a really big Duplo tower. He did his best to get Ben and Damian to join in but they just sat there and stared. As I watched them, I had a feeling that this temporary placement wasn't going to be as easy as I'd first thought. They'd only just arrived but I'd never seen two children so worryingly quiet and blank before.

I knew if there was one thing that helped young children feel secure, it was getting them into a good routine. Especially at night-time when I always gave them a bath and read them a story before bed. I hoped that it would relax Ben and Damian and help them to settle.

'Time for a bath,' I told them. 'I've made it nice and bubbly and put lots of toys in there for you to play with.'

I helped them get undressed. As I lifted Ben's jumper off, I noticed the line of bruises down his arms. I could tell they were a few days old as they were yellowy in colour. I noticed Damian also had bruises on his legs too. Although Clare had already told me about them, it's always a shock to see children's injuries with your own eyes. I still can't comprehend how people can hurt little ones. It made me sad to think that these two were so young but they'd already learnt that adults could cause them pain and upset.

I lifted them gently into the water. They both got in willingly and didn't kick up a fuss, but they just sat there ignoring the toys. I was washing Ben when I noticed his hands looked dirty.

'Oh look at your mucky fingers,' I smiled. 'What have you been up to?'

But as I scrubbed them with the flannel, he flinched in pain. To my horror, I realised that it wasn't dirt, it was purple and black bruises across the top of each knuckle. How the heck had he got those? I didn't want to ask him as it wasn't fair to put such a young child on the spot,

'I'm so sorry if I hurt you,' I said. 'Tell me if it's sore, won't you?'

He nodded. His sad brown eyes stared back at me.

As I got him out and of the bath and gently dried him down, I took a closer look at his hands. All of his fingers were badly bruised and there were painful blisters forming underneath his nails.

I'd knew I'd have to make a note of this in my daily recordings, to pass on to social services. Even if I was looking after a child temporarily, I'd write down any information about their behaviour or things they'd done that day, and those notes went with them when they left. As part of that, I had a drawing of an outline of a body where I could put a cross if I noticed any injuries. As the children had already been examined when they were taken into care, I suspected that social workers already knew about the bruising but it all had to be logged by me too, just to let Clare know.

After their bath I read them a story. Kate had just come home so she popped upstairs to meet them. Afterwards they obediently got into bed.

'Night night,' I told them. 'See you in the morning.'

They didn't respond but rolled over and shut their eyes. The whole time they'd been with me they hadn't said a single word. I went downstairs.

'I don't think you're going to have any trouble from those two,' said Kate. 'They're very quiet and well behaved.'

'I know,' I said. 'Too well behaved if you ask me.'

There was something eerie about it. They were just too quiet. Too compliant.

13

'Hopefully they'll be a bit more responsive tomorrow,' I said. 'It's been a hard day for them.'

Normally when a child first came to live with me I would be grateful for the peace and quiet but this was just plain odd.

TWO

And Baby Makes Three

Normally with under-fives in the house, the first thing you notice is the noise and then the mess. But things were so unbelievably quiet you'd never know that I'd got two little ones living with me. Quiet wasn't even the right word to describe Ben and Damian, they were silent.

They still showed no interest in playing but seemed happy enough to spend the morning following me around while I made beds, picked up toys and got the older two off to school. I chatted away to them, although it was a very one-sided conversation as neither would answer me.

I was glad to talk to someone by the time Clare phoned later that morning.

'You know I mentioned yesterday that Damian and Ben have a six-month-old half-brother?'

'Yes,' I said.

'Well the decision has been made to take Noah into care today and I was wondering whether you'd be prepared to look after him? Obviously just until Pat's better.'

'Of course,' I told her. 'I'd be happy to have him.'

I knew wherever possible it was best to try and keep sibling groups together. I'd fostered babies before so I had a cot already set up in my room and plenty of baby clothes in the cupboards.

'Why have you suddenly decided to remove him now?' I asked.

'As I said yesterday, he doesn't have any physical injuries but we're concerned that it's more emotional neglect with him. You'll see for yourself what I mean when I bring him round,' she said. 'Thanks for being so accommodating, Maggie.'

'No problem,' I said. 'Hopefully it might help the other kids to settle if their brother's here.'

I couldn't wait to tell Ben and Damian about Noah, as I hoped it would provoke some reaction.

'Guess what?' I said. 'Clare's just phoned to tell me that your baby brother is coming to stay here with us too.'

They both looked blankly at me, although I thought I saw a tiny smile from Damian.

Clare turned up a couple of hours later.

'This is Noah,' she said, carrying him into the hallway in his car seat.

I peered down at him and smiled. 'Hello little man,' I said, stroking his cheek.

He was a cute little thing with gorgeous dark curls like his brothers, and deep dark brown eyes that had a similar blankness about them. He was wearing a grubby Babygro with no cardigan or coat but that's not what bothered me. He didn't make a noise or smile at me when I spoke to him. In fact, he didn't react or move at all.

'Is he asleep?' I asked. 'He's so still.'

I'd looked after babies in the past who slept with their eyes open and I thought he might do that.

'No,' said Clare. 'He's just very placid.'

But placid was an understatement. I'd have expected a six-month-old baby to be kicking its legs, smiling or cooing when you spoke to it, or even crying if it was faced with an unfamiliar person like me. But just like his older brothers, Noah stared blankly. It was as if he was looking through me.

'Ben, Damian,' I called, 'your baby brother's here.'

They both came running out into the hallway and their faces broke out into little smiles when they saw Noah. They crowded round his car seat and Ben held his hand.

'It's baby,' smiled Damian in a squeaky voice. 'Our baby.'

I was delighted to hear him speak.

'Do you know, that's the first thing he's said in thirty-six hours,' I told Clare.

She brought Noah into the living room and I took him out of his car seat for a cuddle. He was so stiff it was like holding a toy doll. He didn't relax into my body or snuggle up to me like most babies do when you picked them up. As I stroked his hair, I noticed the back of his head was flat and he had a big bald patch there.

'His head's a very funny shape,' I said.

'Sadly we suspect that he spent most of his time strapped in the car seat or buggy or lying in his cot,' said Clare.

She explained that he wasn't meeting any of his milestones.

'A baby his age should be about to sit up, but Noah's not rolling yet and his neck muscles are very weak from lying down on his back all the time.'

'What made you decide to remove him?' I asked.

'While we don't think that Rob has physically hurt him, he was very controlling over Tracy and I don't think there was much interaction with the baby,' she said.

'Well, we can make sure he gets plenty of that here,' I smiled.

Having fostered many traumatised children over the years, I knew babies were usually the most resilient. Especially babies under a year old who tended to recover quickly and were often left with no memories of early emotional or physical abuse.

'He was checked over by the hospital earlier this week and there were no injuries or bruising, so we didn't think there was a need to get him examined again,' said Clare. 'But if there's anything that concerns you then ring us straight away.'

'I will do,' I said.

'By the way, did he come with anything?'

'Just this,' said Clare, handing me a carrier bag.

Inside was a grubby, stained bottle and a half empty box of formula. They'd both seen better days so I threw them in the bin and made a mental note to send Kate to the shop when she came back from college.

When Clare had gone, I put Noah on my knee and bounced him up and down. Normally a six-month-old baby would love that and would be giggling and smiling, or at least they'd be wriggling and squirming, reaching out and trying to grab my long hair or the necklace I was wearing that day, but Noah did nothing. He didn't smile or cry, just like his brothers he was strangely silent.

'Shall we show him some toys? I said to Ben and Damian. 'I bet he'd like that.'

That morning I'd got a big bag of baby toys out of the loft. I put Noah down on a beanbag while I opened it up and pulled out a rattle shaped like a flower. I kept an eye on him to make sure that he didn't roll off but he didn't move a jot and stayed very still exactly where I'd left him.

'Look at this Noah,' I said, shaking the rattle in front of him. But there was no reaction.

'If you press this button the petals spin round,' I said, showing him. 'And the leaves are all crinkly and crackly.'

He stared back at me. I had thought his brothers were quiet but I'd never seen such blankness in a baby in my life.

I wasn't sure how Noah was going to settle on his first night in a strange place. I wanted to keep everything as calm and as quiet as possible, so I asked Kate to keep an eye on the others while I gave him a bath.

I'd decided to use a baby bath so he felt nice and secure, and I talked to him as I gently took off his Babygro and nappy. He was a chunky little thing and he wasn't malnourished or small for his age, but he had very poor muscle tone and his neck muscles were still very weak.

Most babies tend to grizzle a bit when you undress them, but Noah just lay there obediently. Gently, I lowered him into the warm water. He was very floppy so I had to hold him like a newborn and support his head.

'There you go,' I smiled, squeezing the sponge so the water trickled onto his tummy. 'Is that nice?'

I would have expected a six-month-old to kick their legs or splash the water but he was so still. In fact he didn't react to being in the bath at all, so I had no idea if he was enjoying it. His face remained blank and expressionless.

I'd decided Noah was going to sleep in my room, and so I could keep a close eye on him I'd put the cot by my bed.

Normally it takes babies a few days to settle and get into a routine. Clare had said he was sleeping through, but I was expecting a few broken nights to start off with. After all, he was in a strange place with strange people, away from his parents.

I dimmed the lights, gave him a bottle and then lay him down in the cot.

'Night night, Noah,' I said, bending down to give him a kiss.

I turned the light off, left a night light on and crept out onto the landing. Then I hung around outside the bedroom door and waited for the tears to start when he realised that he'd been left.

But there was nothing.

Not a cry, not a gurgle, not a single noise of any kind.

After five minutes of deafening silence, I crept back into the bedroom just to check that Noah was alright. His eyes were wide open and he was still awake but he was just lying there.

'It's OK,' I soothed. 'Go to sleep.'

I still didn't hear a peep after that. I checked on him every ten minutes and, after an hour of lying there, he was finally asleep. By the time I went to bed, he hadn't moved and was still in the same position lying on his back. I should have been relieved as I'd never had such a young baby settle so well on their first night with me, but I just found it unbelievably odd. He didn't moan, he didn't chatter, he didn't laugh or giggle, and the strangest thing was I hadn't even heard him cry. No, I thought as I drifted off to sleep that night. I'd never fostered a baby like this before.

I woke up the next morning with a start. I had the strangest feeling, a bit like I was being watched, and when I opened my eyes I realised I was right. A pair of huge brown eyes stared at me through the cot bars.

'Good morning, little man,' I said gently. 'When did you wake up?'

It was eerie. How long had he been lying there watching me?

I looked at the clock and was shocked to see it said 8 a.m. I hadn't set my alarm as I'd assumed the baby would wake me up way before my usual 7 a.m. alarm, but even though he was awake, Noah hadn't made a sound.

The rest of the morning was a mad dash as I got everyone up and dressed and did breakfast. Kate had just gone off to college and I was waving Oliver off down the road to school when Clare pulled up outside.

'You're early today. Are you trying to catch me out?' I joked as she came in.

'I thought I'd pop by to see how things are going,' she smiled. 'How's Noah getting on?'

'To be honest, not great,' I said. 'I'm really concerned about him.'

'What do you mean?' she asked.

'I've just never seen a baby like it. He doesn't move, he doesn't reach out, he doesn't babble, he literally does not make a single sound. Clare, he doesn't even cry,' I said. 'Have you ever known a baby that age who doesn't cry?'

His complete lack of interest in life and the world around him was really strange.

'I've never seen a baby that young with such emotional damage before,' I told her. 'I think Pat's got her work cut out with these three kids.'

'Actually, Maggie, it's Pat that I've come to talk to you about,' said Clare hesitantly. 'I'm afraid there's been a bit of bad news.

'The doctors were worried about her chest so they did some tests and unfortunately it turns out she's got pneumonia.'

'Oh no,' I gasped. 'Poor Pat.'

'She's in hospital and she's doing fine, but there's no way she'll be able to foster for a good while until she's better.'

'So,' she paused. 'I was wondering whether you would be able to keep Damian, Ben and Noah until we make a decision about what's going to happen to them long term?'

'OK,' I said. 'But on one condition.'

'Yes?' asked Clare.

'That I can have a health visitor come out to see me today to take a look at Noah. I don't think he's right and I'm worried there's something seriously wrong.'

'I'll sort it ASAP,' she said.

When I come across a child in trouble, like little Noah with his lack of response, or like Ben and Damian's traumatised silence, I see it as a challenge and I go about trying to fix it. This poor little baby needed me and I made it my mission to help him.

Clare kept to her promise and later that day a health visitor called round to see me. I was pleased when I saw it was a lady called Molly, who I'd worked with several times before. She was a real earth mother who'd been doing the job for over twenty years and I really respected her opinion.

'I'm worried about the baby and I just wanted some reassurance,' I told her.

It turned out Molly was the perfect person to speak to. She explained that she'd been involved in the case from the beginning and had been visiting the parents at home.

'The doctors have checked Noah out and I've examined him at home too, and as far as we can see there is nothing medically wrong.'

There was no suspicious bruising or signs of any brain injury.

'Sadly I think it's purely emotional,' she said. She explained that what she'd seen from talking to the parents was that the dad was very controlling with Tracy – limiting her contact with the baby.

'Rob wanted the baby to be in a strict routine,' she said. 'So Tracy was allowed to pick him up to give him a bottle and change him, but after that he was just left.

'He was safe and he wasn't being hurt, but there was no interaction with him and Mum wasn't allowed to pick him up even when he cried.'

'I just can't get over how quiet he is,' I told her.

'Well imagine that every time you cried, you were ignored and left for hours. What would you do?'

'I'd learn not to cry,' I said.

'Exactly,' said Molly. 'You'd realise there's no point making a noise because nothing happens, so instead you just lie there until the next time someone picks you up.'

It was pitifully sad that such a young baby had learnt not to cry and given up communicating with the world. That was an existence, not a life. It was like something out of Third-World orphanage. At six months of age he'd already resigned himself to a life where the only way to get through it was just to lie there.

Poor poor Noah.

'I just hope I can get through to him,' I sighed.

'Of course you can,' said Molly. 'You know as well as I do it's all about play. Lots of play, lots of cuddles, lots of talking. Just throw everything you've got at him, Maggie, and go work your magic.'

'I'll try,' I said.

I don't know whether I felt better or worse after Molly's visit. At least if there was something physically wrong you could see a doctor and try and fix it. Bruises healed, but with emotional damage there was no easy answer.

It was so sad and I was genuinely worried. I'd looked after babies before but I've never seen one with such deep psychological damage. Would I ever be able to get through to him?

THREE

Waving at the Window

I picked up a huge bag of Duplo and tipped it up. There was a satisfying crash as it spilled out all over the living room floor.

'Right let's see what we can build,' I said, getting down on my knees on the carpet which was now a sea of brightly coloured blocks.

If play was what these three needed, play was what they were going to get. I was willing to try anything to encourage them to talk, to make noise and not be afraid to act like children. Noah needed as much stimulation as possible, so I was determined he wasn't going to miss out on the fun. He couldn't sit up yet so I cleared a space and lay him in the middle of the carpet so he could see everything that was going on.

'I think I'm going to build a tower,' I said. 'What does everybody else want to build?'

Neither Ben nor Damian said a word.

'Who'd like to help me?' I asked.

Damian looked down at the floor. Ben shook his head.

'I bet Noah will,' I said.

I pressed some blocks into his little fists and showed him how they banged together to make a noise, but his expression didn't change. Normally with a baby that age their hands would curl around a block and they'd put it straight into their mouth for a good chew. However, he didn't show any interest and the bricks fell to the floor.

'Well if nobody wants to play with me, then I'm going to have to play on my own, I suppose,' I sighed.

For a good hour I built a house, a car, a castle and a boat and continually talked about what I was doing while the children stared at me with their sad, sunken eyes. What on earth were they thinking? Was I even getting through to them? I was just putting the finishing touches to a tower and about to admit defeat when Ben tapped me on the arm.

'What is it, lovey?' I asked.

He gingerly passed me a brick.

'Thank you, Ben,' I said. 'Where would you like me to put that?'

'Top,' he said shyly.

'Where?' I asked.

'On the top,' he said.

'Why don't you do it?' I said.

He shook his head.

'Damian do it?' I asked but he shrank back.

'OK, Maggie will do it.'

I knew from experience that it was all about time and patience. It was about getting the children into a routine and making them feel safe and secure in the hope that eventually I'd be able to bring these frozen little statues to life.

It was just a small step but I was pleased that Ben had passed me the brick and had spoken. The smallest actions can signal the start of bigger changes. However, Noah was still the one who was worrying me the most. He hadn't changed at all yet. I chatted to him continually and was very tactile. I tickled his tummy and stroked his cheek, but still no response.

In a bid to get any sort of engagement from him, I built a huge Duplo bridge right over his belly.

'Look, Noah,' I said, desperate for him to show some interest and reach out for it. 'What's this? Can you see the bridge? Look at all the colours.'

However, there was nothing. No noise, no kicks, no cries. The only way I could tell that he was alive was by the fact that he blinked every now and again, and I could see his little chest going up and down so I knew that he was breathing.

How had these children got like this? Why had they shut themselves down? What were they so afraid of?

I still had so many questions and I was hoping that Clare might be able to answer them when she came round later that morning. She'd promised to update me about what was happening with the investigations into the parents.

'We've had endless discussions with Rob and Tracy,' she said. 'From what I can gather he has a Victorian attitude to children, that they should be seen and not heard. He's extremely dominant and controlling, and it's clear everyone in that flat had to creep around him.'

Clare explained how Ben had told a nursery worker that 'Daddy hit me with some wood'.

'Ben said if he and Damian had been naughty or even made a noise when they were playing then he'd whack their knuckles with a ruler.'

It was absolutely horrifying but it would explain the bruising that I'd seen on Ben's hands in the bath. No wonder the poor boy was scared to pick up a toy.

'What does Rob say about it?' I asked.

'It's hard to determine the truth from him. He's adamant that everything he did was for his children's own good and they just didn't like the fact that he's strict with them. He's denying all knowledge about the bruising and says he doesn't know how it happened.'

'And Mum?' I asked.

'I think Mum's as controlled by Dad as the children, really. She says he's done nothing wrong.'

It was no wonder the children were so timid. They were probably too scared to speak, to put a foot wrong or make a noise in case they were punished. They were frightened to be children.

'I assume the police are involved,' I said.

'Well you know as well as I do, Maggie, that these cases are unlikely to get to court as it's so hard to prove. When social workers went round to the flat to talk to Rob they saw a wooden stick. But Rob's denying ever using it on the kids and says it was there just to teach them a lesson. When social workers tried to ask the children about it, they wouldn't say anything.

'Unfortunately the CPS don't think they've got enough evidence to take it any further. It's Rob's word against that of two young children. And also you've got to question whether it's worth putting them through the trauma of a court case when they're obviously traumatised enough.'

Sadly, I knew she was right

'So what happens now?' I asked.

'The parents have made it clear they want the children back, so we're assessing them to see if that's ever going to be a possibility,' she said. 'At the same time, I think we also need to make plans in case that assessment fails and if that happens then adoption would be best for such young children.'

While Tracy and Rob were being assessed, a court had decided they were allowed supervised contact three times a week at a contact centre.

'A contact worker will come and collect them and take them there and bring them back, so you don't have to worry about it,' Clare told me.

I wasn't sure how the children would react to seeing their mum and stepfather again. Neither Damian nor Ben had mentioned them or asked where they were.

'In the meantime just carry on with the work you're doing with the kids and I'll let you know when a decision has been made about what's going to happen to them long term,' she said. 'Hopefully they'll start to come out of their shells soon.'

'Fingers crossed,' I said.

Thankfully, over the next couple of weeks, Ben and Damian slowly began to respond. Each morning, while I saw Kate off to college and made sure that Oliver had everything he needed for school, I stood the two of them by the front window in the living room and sat Noah next to them in his highchair. It was always a hive of activity first thing outside our house, lots of people coming and going. I pulled the net curtains to one side so they could watch everyone going past while I got the two older ones out of the door. People would walk by and see the three little ones stood there and they'd wave and smile at them. Then

I'd run to the window and we'd all see Kate and Oliver off. We had the same routine every morning.

'Wave bye bye to Kate,' I told them.

I waved although no one else did. Then we'd wave Oliver off down the street when he left for school.

'Bye bye, Ollie,' I said. 'See you this afternoon.'

I even lifted Noah's hand to show him how to wave.

By the end of the first week, much to my delight, Ben and Damian were waving to Oliver and Kate when they left. By the second week they were saying 'Bye bye'.

To me, this was all good progress; every syllable they uttered showed an improvement, a sign of growing confidence. Yet they remained very quiet and obedient. I'd put toys in front of them and they'd look up at me waiting for me to give them permission to touch them, obviously terrified they were going to get told off. I needed to try and get rid of that deep fear they carried from living with their stepfather. I wanted to show Ben and Damian that they now lived in a place where they were allowed to make noise and have fun, and they weren't going to be punished for it.

One afternoon I set some animal figures out on the carpet in the living room. They sat there waiting for my permission to play.

I picked the lion up.

'Well hello Mr Lion,' I said. 'There's some very quiet children here today. What do you think of that?'

Then I let out the loudest roar I could muster.

Ben and Damian both jumped in shock, but thankfully it was followed by a smile.

Then I picked up the horse and started yelling, 'Clippety clop, clippety clop,' as I moved it around the floor.

Damian giggled.

'Who can do the loudest snort?' I said, picking up the pig. 'Can you be a piggy?'

Much to my delight, Ben joined in.

'Oink oink,' he said.

But then immediately afterwards he lowered his head and looked like he was going to burst into tears.

'Sorry for shouting,' he said meekly. 'I didn't mean to.'

'Don't be sorry lovey,' I said. 'You haven't done anything wrong. You're allowed to make noise and be silly in this house.'

As if to prove a point, I picked up a cow.

'Moooo,' I bellowed.

Ben gave me a weak smile. Poor little lad was still terrified he was going to get his knuckles whacked if he put a foot out of place like he had at home. Damian had been quiet up until now, but he loved the little toy ducks and soon he joined in with making quacking noises.

It was helpful having Oliver around as he was a noisy character and he naturally got them involved in his play. When he got home from school one afternoon, he saw Ben holding his car.

'Hey that's mine,' he said.

Ben timidly handed it back to him.

'Why don't you have this one instead,' Oliver told him, handing him a Formula One car. 'Then we can have a race. I bet my car will beat yours.'

Ben didn't seem as fearful around other children, and soon he and Oliver were racing their cars around the carpet. When he heard Oliver making pretend revving noises like a car engine, he joined in too, and Damian clapped and cheered.

The noise was like music to my ears and it was wonderful to hear after the house had been so eerily quiet for the past couple of weeks.

Yet, quietly in the background, Noah continued to be my main worry.

'I've tried everything and nothing seems to be working,' I said to Clare.

'With that level of damage there's not going to be a quick fix,' she said. All you can do is keep persevering and eventually you'll reach him.'

But I just wasn't so sure. While Ben and Damian were slowly coming out of their shells, Noah was still the stiff, silent baby that he'd been when he arrived. I threw every trick in the book at him, every technique that I'd ever learnt over the years since becoming a foster mum.

I knew physical touch was so important so I cuddled him and stroked him. I did lots of rhymes and sang lots of songs, I gently pressed his nose and pretended that it beeped like a car horn, and did 'Round and Round the Garden' endless times. Little children would normally dissolve into giggles when you tickled them under the armpits at the end, but it provoked no response from Noah.

It was the lack of any reaction at all that really unnerved me. One lovely spring afternoon, I took the children out into the garden for a play. I didn't want Noah to miss out so I put a rug in the sandpit and lay him down on it. I moved his hand around in the sand so he could feel the texture of it and experience the grains slipping through his fingers. There was a little baby swing out there and I tied a couple of wind chimes to it and some bells, so it meant that when I put Noah in the swing and pushed him there was lots of noise – but his face never changed.

Tears of frustration pricked my eyes.

'Despite everything I'm doing I just can't reach him,' I said to Kate later on in the kitchen. 'It's like he's just permanently switched himself off from life.'

'If anyone can help him, you can, Maggie,' she said.

I knew it was sweet of her to say and she was being kind but I was starting to question it.

One morning we were running late and, as always, I plonked Noah in his highchair in the front window so he could watch the comings and goings while I went and got Damian and Ben, who were finishing their porridge. When I walked back into the living room to check on him, something made me stop dead in my tracks.

Noah was sat in his highchair but his little hand was reaching out to grab the net curtain that I'd forgotten to pull back. As I went over to him, he turned his head and looked up at me with an annoyed expression on his face as if to say: 'Oi, you haven't done this yet have you?'

It was only a tiny little movement but to me it felt like a miracle had just happened.

'You clever boy!' I smiled, giving him a kiss. 'Silly Maggie hasn't put the curtain up for you, has she, so you can't see out?'

It showed me that he *had* been watching and taking things in. He knew the routine and he'd responded. At last, a breakthrough. It gave me hope that I'd finally got through to him and things were slowly changing. Noah was coming back to life.

FOUR

Breakthrough

After the incident at the window, Noah came on in leaps and bounds. It was the breakthrough he needed and finally I felt like I was getting somewhere with him. In the weeks that followed, he quickly learnt how to roll over, he started kicking his legs when I spoke to him and reaching out for toys.

'He's still not making any noise or smiling, but we're working on that,' I told Clare when she came round.

'I'm sure that will come in time,' she said. 'He's already a very different baby to the one who I brought to your house a few weeks ago.'

There was one thing in particular that I was desperate for him to do.

'I still haven't heard him cry yet,' I told her.

Most people would have thought that was a funny thing to wish for, but when Noah cried I'd truly know that he was well on his way to overcoming the trauma he'd been through in his short little life. He'd been with me for nearly eight weeks and I'd not seen him shed a single tear – unthinkable for a baby of that age.

It was the one thing I couldn't show him how to do. I could talk to him, teach him how to play, encourage him to sit up and crawl, but crying was the one thing that he had to do on his own.

'One step at a time,' Clare told me.

'I know,' I said. 'But that's the one big thing for me that will show he's finally letting go of the past. That he's lost his fear and knows his daddy can't control him anymore.'

'Keep doing what you're doing and it will come,' said Clare.

I hoped to God that she was right.

Ever since Noah had arrived I'd been giving him a bath separately in the baby bath, but he was eight months now and a bit less floppy, so I decided to try him in with Ben and Damian. They were very excited to have their baby brother in the big bath with them. I put them at either end and I sat Noah in the middle, supporting him as he still wasn't sitting up yet.

'Good boy,' I said, gently splashing him with water. 'How do you like that?'

I could tell by the bemused expression on his face that he wasn't sure what to make of it at first. To me that was progress too, as it was better than the perpetual blankness he'd shown at the beginning.

'Why don't you show him some of the toys?' I suggested to Ben and Damian.

We had boats and balls and some little rubber fish that squirted water out of their mouths. Ben dipped one into the bath and filled it up.

'Look Noah,' he said, giving it a squeeze.

Water shot out straight into his face. We all stared at Noah, nervously waiting for his reaction. He blinked furiously as water dripped down his forehead and into his eyes but then, much to all our surprise, a huge radiant smile broke out onto his face.

'Look he liked it!' said Ben, grinning too. 'He's smiling.'

'He certainly is,' I laughed.

'Again!' said Damian. 'Do it again, Ben.'

I don't know whether it was because we were all laughing but the next time he got squirted, Noah grinned and then let out a lovely big chuckle. I was so utterly relieved and happy, it took all my energy not to cry.

'I think that's the best sound that I've ever heard,' I said, swallowing the lump in my throat.

Damian and Ben were jigging around in excitement.

'You're a very clever boy,' I told Noah, tickling him under his chin.

I was so proud of him, in fact I was so proud of all of them and how far they'd come. Just seeing the three of them playing in the bath, not being afraid to have fun and making each other laugh, was amazing.

After the bath I wrapped Noah in a towel and scooped him up in my arms.

'You're really showing us who you are now, aren't you little man?' I said.

As if in response, he nuzzled his little wet head into my neck. It was the first time that he'd really cuddled up to me and shown any affection.

From then on, every night all three of them had a bath together and it was clear Noah loved it. The following evening he kicked his legs and splashed the water with his hands. Three days in there was an even bigger breakthrough when he started making little squeaking noises. It was wonderful to see this passive little baby showing us his personality for the first time.

Ben and Damian were losing their fear too. They had the confidence to play with toys now, but they were still very quiet. I gave them lots of choices, from what fruit they wanted as a snack to what socks and pyjamas they were wearing each day, to try and encourage them to be more vocal. Ben soon got the hang of it and wasn't afraid to express his opinion, but Damian still wasn't saying very much. It was hard, as I knew at home they'd never been given options and no one had been interested in what they thought before. In fact they'd been actively encouraged not to say anything out of a fear of being punished.

As I did every day, one morning I got two jumpers out of Damian's wardrobe.

'Would you like to wear the stripy one or the purple one with a dog on the front?' I asked him.

He looked at me sheepishly and didn't say anything.

'Don't worry there's no right or a wrong answer,' I told him. 'I'm not going to be cross with you. I just want you to tell me what you think.'

But he only shrugged his shoulders.

'OK,' I said. 'If you won't tell me then I'll decide for you. Let's wear the purple one today.'

'No!' Damian shouted, as he saw me taking it off the hanger.

'Don't like purple and don't like doggies. Don't like that jumper. It's scratchy and yuck.'

After his outburst was over he looked up at me and we both burst out laughing.

'Well young man you certainly told me,' I said. 'And thank goodness you did, otherwise I'd have kept on making you wear it.'

I think he'd surprised himself, but it was wonderful to hear him finding his voice and expressing his opinion for the first time.

'In fact,' I smiled. 'If you really, really don't like this jumper shall we just throw it in the bin?'

Damian grinned.

'What are you doing?' asked Ben, as he saw me marching outside to the bin.

'We're throwing this jumper away, Ben, because Damian doesn't like it. He doesn't like the colour or the dog on the front and it's itchy apparently.'

He looked at me like I was mad, but I wanted to do something dramatic to prove to Damian that I was listening to him, that I valued his opinion and that it was OK to speak out.

What made me realise how far the children had come was when they'd go off for contact with their parents. Three times a week a contact worker called Alison would come to pick them up and take them to a contact centre to see Tracy and Rob. There would be activities for them to do and toys set out for them to play together and sometimes they'd bake cakes or make lunch. It was a chance for them to see each other, and also for social workers to observe Rob and Tracy interacting with the kids and see how they coped with them.

None of the children ever kicked up a fuss about going and they always trotted off obediently with Alison, but every time they came back they were exceptionally quiet. As time went on I could see the effect it was having on Noah, especially.

One afternoon Alison dropped him home and when she put his car seat down in the hallway, my heart sank. I took one look at his little face and realised the blank little baby that he'd been when he first arrived was back. His eyes were glazed and he was sat there silently as if he was in a trance not reacting to anything.

I panicked. Was seeing his birth parents destroying all the progress he'd made and taking him back to square one?

'Kate, will you keep an eye on the others for me,' I said, taking Noah through to the kitchen.

Damian and Ben were playing happily now they were back, Noah was the one I was most concerned about. I sat down at the kitchen table and put him over one shoulder with his bottom resting on the dining table. I cuddled him, stroked his back and talked to him in a gentle voice. I said the silliest things, in fact I was just spouting nonsense really.

'Look at those beautiful daffodils in the vase. I love daffodils. They're so bright and cheery with their lovely yellow colour. I must put some more water in there so they last a bit longer or I'll have to buy some more from the shop.'

I knew it didn't matter what I was saying. What mattered was that Noah heard the low, soft tone of my voice and felt the warmth of my body next to him. I cuddled him and talked to him for almost an hour until I felt him start to wriggle about and pull on my necklace. When I looked at him he gave me a weak smile and I could see the life had come back into his eyes again and the fear had gone.

Alison the contact worker had noticed it too.

'The kids are so, so quiet at contact,' she said. 'They don't play with any toys or talk, they just sit there. But the minute I turn the car into your street Ben and Damian start chatting to each other. If it's OK, it would be useful for me to see what they're like at home with you.'

'Of course,' I said. 'Why don't you come in one morning before you drop them off and you can see for yourself?'

Alison took me up on my offer. A few days later she came in for fifteen minutes before she had to take the children. We had a cup of tea while the children played. Damian was tipping out all the toys looking for a transformer and Ben was noisily chugging a train around the living room, while Noah was pressing the buttons on a toy phone and laughing when it made a noise.

'Wow,' she said. 'They're like completely different kids. At contact, they really have to be pushed to play with toys and you don't hear a peep out of them.'

'It shows the control their dad still has over them,' I said. 'It probably brings back all their old fears, and they're scared that if they make a noise or annoy Dad then he'll punish them, so they revert back to being quiet.'

I was wondering how the assessment of their parents was going, until Clare answered the question for me a few days later.

'Rob's been aggressive to one of the social workers during contact and we feel like he's affecting the mood of the sessions,' she said. 'So we've decided that Rob and Tracy will have separate sessions with the children.'

On the day of Rob's first solo session, Alison came round to collect the kids as normal. However, half an hour later they were back.

'I'm afraid he didn't turn up,' she said.

Thankfully Noah was too young to understand and the other two seemed OK with it. After that, to avoid the same thing happening again, Rob was told the children wouldn't come to the contact centre until after he'd arrived. He needed to be there fifteen minutes before the session started so Alison could phone me and let me know that it was happening. It meant that our day was on hold until just after 10 a.m., and no phone call meant no contact, but it was better than having them waiting around at the centre for their dad to turn up.

However, the phone call never came because Rob didn't turn up for any of his sessions.

Clare came round to update me.

'We've made the decision to stop all contact with Dad,' she said. 'Social workers have tried going round to the flat to talk to him about the implications of this, but he's not there and doesn't call them back.

'If someone's not willing to turn up for contact then he's effectively pulling out of the assessment. He knows that he's not going to get the children back.'

It was Tracy I really felt for. Now it was up to her to decide what she wanted to do. If she stayed with Rob she would never see her children again. But if she left him then there was the possibility that they might be able to come back and live with her.

'Mum still wants to carry on with contact,' Clare told me.

Who knew what would happen. Without the controlling influence of Rob around, maybe she could be a good mother to the children. They hadn't been malnourished or dirty when they'd first been taken into care and they didn't come back from seeing her in the same timid state they did when they saw their dad.

Sadly, after two contact visits, Tracy stopped coming too. Perhaps it was pressure from Rob that had made her pull out of the assessment. Whatever the reasons, it was clear now there was only one way forward for the children – adoption.

FIVE

A Cry in the Dark

It was the middle of the night and a strange noise disturbed me from my sleep. I sat bolt upright in bed, my heart racing.

It was a loud wailing sound.

What the heck is it?

As I started to come round, I realised it was coming from right next to me. From the cot.

And then suddenly it clicked.

'Oh my goodness, Noah,' I laughed. 'It's you. You're crying!'

I turned on the light and peered into his cot. He was sat there with an angry look on his face, tears streaming down his cheeks.

'What is it my love?' I said, picking him up and stroking his hair. 'Are you hungry? Is that what it is? Or did you just want a cuddle?'

It was the first time that he'd ever woken up in the night before. He was very cross and his angry wails got louder and louder, but I couldn't wipe the smile off my face. I don't think I'd ever been so happy to hear a baby cry before. For the past three months I'd been desperate to hear this sound.

A few minutes later, a bleary-eyed Kate waddled into my bedroom in her dressing gown, rubbing her pregnant belly.

'What's that horrible noise, Maggie?' she said.

None of us were used to hearing a baby cry, so it was a shock.

'It's Noah,' I said, delighted. 'He's crying. Isn't that amazing?'

'Not really,' she said, looking at me like I'd gone mad. 'Can't you shut him up? I'm trying to sleep.'

'No, I won't,' I said. 'It's wonderful that he's found his voice.'

She tutted and shuffled off back to bed.

I couldn't have been any happier if I'd won the lottery, and I must admit I couldn't resist indulging Noah a bit. I cuddled him, gave him a bottle and even though it was 3 a.m. we had a little play. I wanted him to know that when he cried now, someone was listening and would respond with lots of love and affection. Eventually he fell asleep in my arms and gently I put him back down in his cot.

I couldn't get back to sleep after that, but it didn't matter. I lay there, exhausted but happy and also very, very relieved. He was finally behaving like a normal baby should. It was wonderful that he felt secure and relaxed enough to cry again, and it confirmed that he had the ability to recover from what had happened to him at home which was what had concerned me most. I knew his emotional damage was healing at last.

Now Noah had found his voice there was no stopping him. Whenever he didn't like something he'd certainly let us know about it by letting rip with a loud wail. It took me a few days to get used to the noise. It was as if crying for the first time opened the floodgates and suddenly reminded him that he was alive. He progressed so much over the next few weeks – he learnt how to wave and started to babble.

I was in the kitchen preparing dinner one afternoon when Oliver came running in.

'Maggie, Maggie, come quickly,' he yelled.

Thinking there was something horribly wrong, I threw down the knife I was chopping carrots with and ran through to the living room.

'What is it?' I gasped. 'What's happened?'

'Look,' said Ben proudly. 'Look what Noah's doing.'

I looked over to where he was pointing to see Noah proudly crawling around the carpet with a big grin on his face.

'He can do crawling,' smiled Damian, clapping his hands with glee.

Much to all our amazement, Noah stopped crawling, sat up and started clapping his hands too.

'Well aren't you a clever boy?' I said.

'Babba, da da da,' he replied, as if he knew exactly what he was saying.

A few days later, Molly the health visitor came round to give Noah a routine check. She hadn't seen him for a couple of months and she was gob smacked at his progress.

'I honestly can't believe it,' she said, as she struggled to keep him still so she could weigh and measure him. 'He's like a different baby. You really have worked wonders here, Maggie.'

'It's not rocket science,' I told her. 'I've just talked to him, played with him and shown him lots of love, and he's done the rest.'

'Well you've done him proud,' she said. 'He's a happy healthy little lad.'

Afterwards he was full of smiles and giggles as Molly rolled a soft ball to him. He'd caught up with his development, his body was growing normally and he was meeting all the milestones for a nine-month-old.

'The icing on the cake was when he cried for the first time the other night,' I told her. 'That's when I knew I'd really got through to him.'

'It's funny how all this progress has happened after the contact with his birth parents stopped,' she said.

I hadn't thought about the timing of it, yet I realised that she was right. A sad situation, but perhaps not seeing his biological parents had meant he finally felt safe, secure and loved and he could finally move on.

Noah finding his voice also helped Ben and Damian too. It allowed them to be noisy as well. They watched how I reacted when he cried, and they could see I wasn't angry or telling him off, so it gave them permission to be noisy too. They really came out of their shells and were chattering all the time, and not frightened to make noises when they played. A lovely bond was also developing between the three of them. Kate and I were sat on the sofa one afternoon while the three of them played on the floor. Noah shouted something in his baby talk that sounded like gobbledygook, but Ben and Damian obviously understood as they went scampering off to bring him a toy. They did this again and again, and if Noah liked what they'd brought him then he'd smile, but if he didn't he'd throw the toy across the carpet with a grumpy look on his face.

'He's the noisiest and the bossiest out of the three of them,' said Kate with a smile. 'He's running rings around the other two.'

'I know,' I said. 'I can't believe how much progress he's made. It's a complete turnaround.'

Clare was also pleased with how things were going.

'I think it's time for me to start putting feelers out to see if there are any potential adopters who might be interested in taking on the children,' she said.

That meant we had to tell them what was happening. I knew Noah was too young to understand but I wasn't sure how Ben and Damian were going to react to the news. She sat them all down in the living room and they perched on my knee.

'Now Clare's got something very important and exciting to tell you,' I said. 'So you need to listen very carefully.'

'As you know, you don't live with your mummy and daddy anymore so I'm going to look around for a really special new mummy and daddy for you,' she told them.

Neither Damian nor Ben showed any reaction at all.

'OK,' said Ben. 'Can I go and play with my train now?'

Clare and I nodded.

'Me come too,' said Damian, jumping off my knee and following him.

They both seemed as equally nonplussed as each other.

'They seemed to take that OK,' said Clare, when we went to have a chat in the kitchen.

'Hmm, I'm worried they're still conditioned by their dad, and they're just too compliant and too accepting of everything,' I told her.

I hoped they'd accepted it and understood it as much as a three and four-year-old could.

'Will you try and organise a goodbye with their birth parents?' I asked.

46

When children were adopted, saying goodbye to their biological parents was encouraged so there was no confusion and worry or hope about whether they would ever have to go back and live with them. It was an important thing to do to allow kids to move on.

'We've already offered both Rob and Tracy the chance to say goodbye to the kids, but neither of them wanted to take us up on that,' she said sadly.

I've heard it many times before, but it has always shocked me that some parents can completely remove themselves from their kids without even so much as a goodbye.

I'd prepared myself for the fact that it might take a while to find potential adopters, as it was often tricky to place a large sibling group. Even now that Pat had recovered, it was best that the children had stayed with me. So I was surprised when Clare phoned me the following week.

'There's a couple interested in the children and to be honest, Maggie, they sound absolutely perfect,' she told me.

'Wow, that was quick,' I said.

She explained Linda and Dave were both teachers in their late thirties and had been married for seven years. They lived in a town a couple of hours' drive away from us.

'They've had countless rounds of IVF which didn't work,' she said. 'They're not fazed by the idea of three children as they're desperate for a ready-made family and they're happy to take on a sibling group.'

Linda was dual heritage, which was ideal as children were generally tried to be placed with parents whose ethnic background reflected their own.

It all sounded too good to be true.

'What I need to do now is come round and do a proper assessment of each child, so I can tell Linda and Dave all about them, what they're doing and what they like and dislike,' said Clare.

Later that week she came round to spend a few hours observing the children. Noah was having a nap but Clare and I sat in the front room and chatted to Ben and Damian while they played.

'What do you like doing?' she asked them.

'My best game is Lego,' said Ben. 'And Playmobil.'

'And I like jumping,' said Damian, showing us how far he could jump.

'I like doing hopping,' shouted Ben.

It was really sweet to see the pair of them showing off by hopping and jumping around the room.

'It's lovely to see how much self-confidence they've got and how chatty they are,' she said. 'It's such a turnaround from how they were when they first arrived.'

Clare took a few photos of them but she was very careful not to mention the adopters. It was such early days and we didn't tell the children until further down the line when the potential parents had been approved.

When Noah woke up we all had lunch together. He sat in his highchair, grinning at Clare, blowing raspberries and chomping on cucumber, pepper and carrot sticks.

'He's really come on,' said Clare. 'I'll tell Linda and Dave how delightful and happy these children are and I don't think they're going to be able to resist.'

I hoped she was right.

Clare was going to go and see them the following week and let me know. I had everything crossed that it went well.

*

'How did it go?' I asked.

'It was brilliant,' she said. 'They're really lovely people. I spent the morning with them and gave them lots of information about the children and showed them all the photographs.

'As we'd hoped they really seemed taken with them,' she said. 'The good news is they called me back this morning and said they didn't need any more time to think about it and they definitely want to go ahead with it. Are you pleased?'

'Of course I am,' I said. 'I'm delighted, it's just very quick.'

I really was chuffed. Of course I was sad that Damian, Ben and Noah would be leaving, as we all loved them and they'd become a big part of our family. But I had to focus on the positives. They deserved a permanent family of their own. Whenever children have a long-term shot at happiness, I have to let them go. And then I have to make room for the next ones. That's just the way it is for a foster carer.

'The matching panel's at the end of this month, so all being well the children could be moving to their home within the next couple of months,' Clare said.

I just hoped the kids would be able to cope with the big changes coming their way.

SIX

New Life

Dimming the lights, everyone started to sing as I carried the cake across the kitchen.

'Happy birthday to you, happy birthday to you. Happy birthday dear Noah . . .'

He gave a big gummy smile as I put the chocolate cake down on the tray of his highchair.

'. . . happy birthday to you.'

'Blow out your candle,' said Oliver.

Noah stared in amazement at the flickering flame, unsure what to make of it all.

'Ben and Damian give him a hand and show him what to do,' I said.

They each gave a few puffs and we all cheered and clapped as the candle was finally blown out.

It was Noah's first birthday and we were having a little tea party at home. As I watched him shovel a huge slice of chocolate cake into his mouth with his fists, I could see he was enjoying being the centre of attention.

Afterwards, Ben and Damian helped him to rip the wrapping paper off his presents. There was a guitar that lit up and played music when you pressed the buttons, a wooden train with blocks that stacked on the back and lots of board books.

'Look at all those lovely toys,' I said. 'Just think you'll be able to take them with you to your new mummy and daddy's house.'

That was more for Ben and Damian's benefit. We hadn't told the children about Linda and Dave yet but for the past few weeks I'd talked a lot about new mummies and daddies and we'd read stories about children being adopted.

In three days' time the couple were due to go in front of a matching panel. The panel was made up of a dozen independent people who would look at the reports from Social Services, speak to Clare and then Linda and Dave, and decide whether or not it was a good match. I'd known couples be turned down by a panel or been told they weren't ready to adopt a child yet, and it was never guaranteed.

So on the day I was a bag of nerves waiting to hear if they'd been given the green light. Finally, just before lunchtime, Clare rang.

'It all went well, Maggie,' she said. 'Linda and Dave and the kids have been matched and everyone's delighted.'

'That's wonderful news,' I sighed. 'What a relief.'

'I'll pop round tomorrow to chat to the children and bring them some pictures of their new parents.'

I wasn't too concerned about how the kids were going to react to the news. I knew they would be fine because they had each other. Wherever they went they would be together and they'd get comfort from that. Up until now, neither Ben nor Damian had ever mentioned their birth parents. I'd found that was normal for younger children. If where they were living now

51

was better than where they'd come from, then they tended not to ask for them, especially as they didn't see their birth parents any more. However, I always had a flutter of nerves when such life-changing news like this was being broken, as children sometimes surprised you with their reactions.

Clare came over the next morning. I sat Damian and Ben down at the kitchen table and put Noah on my knee.

'I've got some very good news to tell you,' said Clare gently. 'I've found you a lovely new mummy and daddy.'

Neither of them said anything right away but I could see them slowly taking in the news.

'Will this mummy be a new mummy or a new, new mummy?' Ben asked with a puzzled look on his face.

I think by 'new mummy' he meant his birth mother Tracy.

'This will be a new, new mummy lovey,' I told him. 'You haven't met her yet but she can't wait to meet you as she's heard a lot about you.'

'Is Noah coming to live with them too?' asked Damian.

'Of course,' I said. 'All three of you are going. I think they'd be very sad if Noah didn't come too.'

That seemed to reassure them.

'And guess what?' said Clare. 'I've got some photos of your new mummy and daddy. Would you like to see them?'

They both nodded their heads excitedly.

'My new mummy's pretty,' said Damian with a smile, as he studied the pictures.

'Can my new bedroom be red?' asked Ben.

'I don't know,' said Clare. 'But what you can do is ask your new mummy and daddy because they're coming round to see you tomorrow.'

They appeared to have accepted the news and it had gone as well as it could.

'They seem happy,' said Clare. 'Only time will tell, but hopefully we won't have any problems.'

'They're good kids,' I said. 'My only fear is that they revert back to how they were when they first arrived.'

I was worried that if the children felt anxious or insecure about the move then they would go back to their old quiet ways and stop speaking.

However, they seemed at ease with what was happening. Clare had made lots of copies of the photos of Linda and Dave so we put them up all over the house and the kids wanted one in their bedroom.

'Night night new mummy and daddy,' we said before they went to sleep that night.

The next morning, Linda and David came round with Clare. I could see they were nervous, but they were very warm and friendly and I could tell by their faces they were besotted by the kids already.

I took them into the living room with the children and they sat on the settee. Any worries I'd had about the kids shutting down and going silent melted away. They were their usual, noisy, happy selves and all three of them giggled as they rolled around the floor together. Damian piled on top of Ben and, not wanting to miss out on the action, Noah crawled over to them and climbed on the top of Damian's back.

'They're lovely,' smiled Linda. 'They're so full of personality, especially the baby.

'He's a real live wire. You'd never believe that he was the one who was the most damaged, would you?' I said.

'From everything I've read and heard from Clare, you really have done a great job with them,' she said. 'You must be so proud of them.'

And as I watched them all playing noisily, perhaps a little bit too noisily at times, I couldn't have been more proud of them if they had been my own.

I liked Linda and Dave instantly. It's hard to explain exactly what it was but they just felt right. Dave had kind blue eyes and a gentle, quiet nature, and Linda was very genuine and smiley. Both of them had an underlying warmth to them.

They didn't overwhelm the children by jumping in and demanding their attention. They sat back and allowed the kids to come to them in their own time. I could see Ben and Damian were intrigued, and they kept looking over and smiling shyly.

'Are you our new new mummy and daddy?' asked Ben.

Dave smiled.

'Yes,' he said.

'OK,' said Ben, and went off and carried on playing.

A little while later, he picked up some toy cars and squeezed himself in between Linda and Dave on the sofa. It was as if that gave Damian permission to approach them, and he came over to show them his teddies. When it was time for Noah's bottle, I plonked him on Linda's lap and handed the bottle to her. She looked a little surprised at first, but soon Noah was happily nestled in her arms, gulping down his milk.

Both she and Dave seemed natural with the kids, and it all felt very relaxed. They stayed a couple of hours the first day and I couldn't have been more pleased with the way it had gone.

*

The settling in was due to take place over a week, and each day Linda and Dave would spend a little bit more time with the children. The next day they stayed for lunch and they put Noah down for his afternoon nap in his cot. The following day they took the children to the park and the day after that they stayed for dinner and gave the children a bath and put them to bed. I was always floating around in case they needed me, however the children didn't seem to need any reassurance. I didn't have to persuade them to go to Dave and Linda instead of me, it naturally happened. Ben and Damian looked happy and, after only a few days, Noah had formed a strong bond with them.

He'd started to pull himself up to a standing position now and while he was coasting along the furniture one afternoon, he stumbled and banged his mouth on the coffee table. He collapsed to the floor and burst into floods of tears. My natural instinct was to leap up and comfort him, but I had to stop myself and let Linda and Dave take over. In the end, I didn't need to as Noah went to them.

He crawled over to the sofa where Linda was sitting and held his arms up to her. It was lovely to see how surprised and pleased she was that he'd sought her out, and she looked like she was going to burst into tears as she scooped him up in her arms.

'It's OK, Noah,' she soothed. 'You're OK my darling.'

She stroked the little curls on the back of his head and I could tell that she was savouring every minute of the feeling of his little warm body cuddling up to her.

Dave sat there watching.

'We've waited a long time for this,' he told me with tears in his eyes.

I could see how much it meant to them that they were finally going to be someone's mummy and daddy.

'Well if the past few days are anything to go by, I think you're all going to be very happy together,' I smiled.

On the day before the children were due to leave, they went with Linda and Dave to spend the day at their house and take their things over. I'd arranged to spend the day shopping for baby things with Kate. She was only a couple of weeks away from her due date now and we needed to get organised. Even though I had a house full of baby stuff, I wanted to get her new things especially for her. As the months had passed, I'd got over my initial shock about her pregnancy and now I was starting to look forward to the idea of a new baby.

'I wonder how the kids are getting on at their new house,' I sighed, looking at my watch.

'They'll be fine,' she said. 'They seem really happy and excited.'

I knew she was right. As far as introductions went, it couldn't have gone any more smoothly.

It was a long drive from Linda and Dave's back to our house, and when they got home that night they were tired but happy. Noah had fallen asleep in the car and the other two were already bathed and in their pyjamas, so I put them straight into bed. Dave carried them upstairs and I tucked them in.

'Just think when you wake up in the morning you're going to live with your new mummy and daddy,' I told them, and they both gave me a sleepy smile.

That night I stayed up late to put the finishing touches to their memory boxes. They were three little wooden boxes the size of shoe boxes that I'd written their names on and filled with mementoes from their time with us – photographs, little toys they'd enjoyed playing with, leaflets from any places that we'd visited and lots of photographs. I'd chosen things they could look at in years to come that would help them connect their memories and remember living with us.

I had one last little look through Noah's. There was the flower rattle that I'd tried to get him interested in when he'd first arrived, his first birthday cards and a little teddy I'd bought him. However, it was seeing the tatty little Babygro that he'd arrived in that got me the most. I had a lump in my throat as I remembered the silent, blank little baby that he'd been, compared to the smiley, noisy little lad he was now. It made me realise how far they'd come and how much I was going to miss them.

No matter how many times I'd done it over the years, saying goodbye to children never got any easier.

The next morning we'd arranged for the children to leave early so Oliver could wave them off before he went to school. He was going to miss them too, so I knew that it was important for him to say goodbye.

I am a firm believer that no matter how sad I feel inside, big, emotional goodbyes aren't helpful for children, so I always try to keep things positive and upbeat.

'I'll see you soon,' I told them as I gave each of them a cuddle and a kiss.

'I don't know what to say, but thank you so, so much,' said Linda.

'You've got my number,' I told her. 'Stay in touch and if you need anything just let me know.'

Oliver, Kate and I stood on the doorstep and watched as they got the kids into their car seats. As the engine started up,

Ben and Damian waved, and I could see Noah's chubby little face smiling through the window at me. I blew kisses at them as they drove away.

'Right we'd better get you off to school young man,' I said to Oliver, hurrying inside before he could see that my cheeks were wet with tears.

I always feel a bit low for a few days when children leave. Ben, Damian and Noah had only been with us for a few short months but I'd grown to love all three of them. I tried to put on a brave face in front of Kate and Oliver as I knew they felt it too.

That first morning I kept myself busy, stripping beds and giving everywhere a good clean, but as I walked into my bedroom and saw the empty cot, I couldn't hold my emotions back any more. I sat on the bed and had a good weep.

Kate, bless her, knew that cleaning was my way of coping so she kept out of my way for most of the day. Later on, she brought me up a cup of tea.

'The house is going to seem so quiet without them,' I sighed.

'Well it won't be for long,' said Kate, rubbing her huge bump. 'You'll be wishing for peace again when there's a crying newborn keeping us all awake.'

'I can't wait,' I smiled.

As it turned out I didn't have to wait very long. Forty-eight hours after the children had left, Kate woke me up in the night to tell me she'd gone into labour twelve days early. I rushed her to the local hospital and, after a three-hour labour, I was holding her hand as she pushed a beautiful baby boy called William into the world. My stomach muscles were aching by the end of it as I think I was pushing with her.

I held him in my arms for the first time and his little fist curled around my finger.

'I'm so proud of you,' I told her. 'He's absolutely perfect.'

Having a baby in the house again was lovely and it took my mind off missing the children. William was a noisy boy from day one and kept us all awake with his crying. It did make me think about how different Noah was at first though.

A month after the children had left we all went round to visit them at their new home and took baby William along to meet them.

'We've got a surprise for you,' said Linda when she came to the door.

She showed me into the living room where Noah was toddling around, a big beam on his face.

'He started walking last week,' she said proudly. 'We took him to get his first pair of shoes today.'

The shop had taken a photograph of him in his new blue shoes which now had pride of place on the mantelpiece. I was so pleased that her and Dave had been the ones to see Noah reach that milestone. Little things like that are so important and would have made them feel like proper parents.

'How have they been?' I asked.

'They're doing brilliantly,' she beamed. 'It's strange but it feels like they've always been here.'

All three of them were happy to see us and, importantly, were equally as happy to wave us off after we'd been there a couple of hours. They were comfortable and settled in their new home; we were just a small chapter in their lives going forward.

As we drove home that night, I felt really content. Ben, Damian and Noah had found their forever family and got their happy ending. I thought about how much little lives can change with love and perseverance. There isn't a smooth path to happiness for most of the children I look after, but time is a great healer. And as I looked at William fast asleep in his car seat with his tiny fists curled up around his head, I wondered who would be coming along to join our little family next.

A Family for Christmas

ONE

A Tragic Accident

Fostering is my vocation and there's nothing I like more than welcoming children into my home and giving them love and stability. But believe me I'm no Mother Theresa. Like any parent, by the end of the six-week summer break I was tearing my hair out.

The holidays had been lovely but, boy, they were long and I was fed up with the endless squabbling. To be honest, I'd started counting down the days until September when the two girls that I fostered could go back to school.

Louisa was fifteen and she'd been living with me for the past three years, ever since her parents had died in a car crash. When she first came to me she was painfully shy and struggling to cope with her grief. But slowly she'd come out of her shell and she had a good circle of friends that she could confide in.

Over the past year or so she'd turned into a typical mono-syllabic, sullen teenager, and she was currently going through a 'Goth' phase. She'd dyed her long, straight brown hair black and had taken to wearing heavy black eyeliner, although I only allowed her to do that at weekends and holidays, when she wasn't in school.

Then there was six-year-old Lily, who had arrived around the same time. She'd been taken into care because her father was a violent alcoholic but her mother refused to leave him. She looked like a little angel with her golden curls and big blue eyes, but her behaviour had been far from angelic at first. She had terrible temper tantrums and had even smashed furniture, such was the force of her anger. Thankfully her behaviour had been much more settled since she had come to live with me.

The girls usually got along brilliantly, but as the weeks had gone by the bickering had increased, and I could see they both needed the stimulation and routine of school back in their lives. I'd realised I did too, and when the first day of the new term came around I think it was a relief to all of us. Shiny new shoes had been purchased, school bags had been packed with brand new stationery, and now I was ready to wave them both off.

'Have you got everything?' I asked Louisa.

'Yes,' she sighed.

'Well have a good first day back and I'll see you tonight.'

'I will,' she said, as the front door slammed behind her.

She was starting year eleven which meant she'd be doing her GCSEs, so it was a big year for her.

After she'd gone there was just Lily to get ready. She was still in primary school so I dropped her off every day.

'Maggie I don't want to go,' she wailed, as I ran a brush through her blonde curly hair and tied it back in a bobble.

'You'll be fine,' I told her. 'You love school and you'll get to see all your friends again.'

I remembered that tummy-churning mixture of nerves and excitement that you always felt on the first day of a new term no matter how old you were.

After swapping pleasantries with the other mums and giving Lily's hand a reassuring squeeze before she went into her new classroom, I finally headed home. As I walked through the front door, I breathed a sigh of relief. I flicked the kettle on to make myself a cup of tea and flopped down at the kitchen table.

Bliss.

I was on my own for the first time in six long weeks and it felt wonderful. However, it was short-lived. I took one gulp of my tea when the shrill ring of the home phone shattered my peace.

'Hi Maggie, I'm not interrupting anything am I?' said a voice I recognised as Rachel, my supervising social worker from the local authority.

'Just the first proper sit down and hot cup of tea I've had in the past six weeks,' I joked. 'But don't worry, I won't hold that against you.'

Rachel and I had worked together for years and we knew each other well enough to enjoy a bit of banter.

'I've got a bit of an unusual case that I wanted to chat to you about,' she said.

That sparked my interest straight away.

'Go on then,' I said, taking a quick sip of tea. 'You know I'm a sucker for unusual. Tell me more.'

'There's the possibility that we have a baby boy who might need to be placed,' she said.

A Family for Christmas

My ears pricked up at the mention of a baby. My last placement had been with Ruth – a nine-year-old who'd been sexually abused by her father, who'd thankfully gone to prison for his crimes. It had been emotionally draining supporting her through the trauma of a court case, but happily Ruth had been reunited with her birth mother whom she'd now gone to live with. Her behaviour had been challenging, to say the least, and it had been hard on Lily and Louisa at times. I liked to vary the ages of the children that I fostered and I knew the girls loved babies.

'Where's he coming from?' I asked.

'Well, it's unusual because it's not a neglect case and he's not being taken into care,' said Rachel. 'All I know is that it's a one-year-old boy who was involved in an accident and has been left with disabilities.

'He's still in hospital and the doctors have said he's well enough to be discharged, but from what I can gather the parents aren't coping so Social Services has offered to help.'

'What happened to him?' I asked.

'That I don't know I'm afraid,' said Rachel. 'I said I would ask to see if you were interested, and if you are then I can arrange for you to meet up with the hospital social worker who's dealing with it.'

'Yes,' I said. 'I'd definitely be interested.'

I was intrigued. Disabilities didn't bother me at all and I wanted to find out more about this little boy and what had happened to him.

'Like I said, nothing is definite at this point,' Rachel told me. 'The hospital is working with the parents to discuss various options.'

'That's absolutely fine,' I said. 'I won't get my hopes up.'

It didn't take long for the hospital social worker to get in touch. Fifteen minutes after I'd put down the phone to Rachel, a lady called Julie rang.

'It would be better to meet you face to face so I can tell you more,' she said. 'Could you come up to the hospital for a chat?'

'Yes, of course,' I said.

'We need to move quickly. Is there any chance you could pop up to the children's ward this morning?'

'No problem,' I told her.

My plan had been to tidy up my bombshell of a house, but that could wait. The hospital was only half an hour's drive from me so I was up there by mid-morning. A woman who I assumed was Julie was waiting for me at reception.

'Nice to meet you, Maggie,' she said, shaking my hand. 'I've heard a lot of good things about you.'

I wondered if she was going to take me onto the ward to meet the baby or his parents, but she led me into an office.

'So, as Rachel will hopefully have explained, the circumstances are unusual,' she said. 'We're potentially looking for someone to foster a one-year-old boy called Edward. I'm afraid it's a really tragic case.'

I listened as she explained how Edward and his mum, Sheila, were in the garden at home one afternoon.

'Edward was sat on a rug on the grass playing with his toys, when the doorbell rang,' she said.

'He seemed happy, so Sheila left him there and ran to the front door to answer it. It was the postman with a parcel. She could only have been gone two or three minutes at the most, but when she came back outside, she found Edward floating

A Family for Christmas

face down in their fishpond. He'd just learnt to walk and must have toddled over and fallen into the water.'

'Oh no, how awful,' I said, feeling sick to my stomach at how traumatic that must have been for her. It was every parent's worst nightmare.

'Sheila was hysterical,' explained Julie. 'She pulled him out and a neighbour heard her screaming and called an ambulance.'

The paramedics had managed to resuscitate him, and at the hospital he was put on life support. Much to everyone's amazement, slowly he started to get stronger and after a few weeks he started to pull through.

'Even though he'd been taken off life support the doctors were still very concerned as he was very weak,' said Julie. 'His brain had been starved of oxygen for so long and they didn't know what damage had been done, but they warned his mum and dad that his quality of life was likely to be very poor.'

'Those poor, poor parents,' I sighed, my eyes filling with tears.

Their son had miraculously pulled through but at what cost?

'None of the medical staff could believe that he'd survived,' said Julie. 'And as the weeks passed, he got stronger and stronger. He's been in hospital eight weeks now and he's still holding his own. His breathing is fine, he was tube fed but now he's able to suck on a bottle, and he's just started to take a few mouthfuls of solid food.'

It was incredible that this little boy had defied all the odds and pulled through. But unfortunately it wasn't the fairy-tale ending everyone had desperately wanted.

'After everything that he's been through, Edward is badly brain damaged and he has been left with cerebral palsy,' said Julie.

'Unfortunately, nobody can predict what's going to happen to him in the future or know the extent of the damage at this stage. From a medical point of view, there's no more the hospital can do now. It's just a case of watching and waiting to see how he develops.'

'And how are his parents?' I asked.

Julie shrugged.

'As you can imagine, they're in a terrible state. They've hardly eaten or slept for the past couple of months. Sheila's spent every night at the hospital.'

I couldn't even begin to imagine the emotional roller coaster they'd been on.

'Emotionally, they're wrung out,' said Julie. 'I think they just need to a bit of space and time to come to terms with what's happened.

'I got involved because the doctors could see that they weren't coping. I've had many long, tearful discussions with Sean and Sheila, and they just don't feel ready to take Edward home yet. They're worried they won't be able to care for him, but medically he's ready to be discharged.

'There's also a lot of guilt there. Sheila blames herself for what happened to her son and she's worried that Sean blames her too.'

My heart went out to his poor woman. Nobody's perfect and we all make split second decisions that are perhaps not the right ones. But hers had changed all of their lives forever.

'The sad thing is Edward is an identical twin,' said Julie. 'His brother Andrew was at the supermarket with his grandma when it happened. So every day his parents see him and it must bring it home to them what they've lost.'

It was gut wrenchingly sad to think what this family must be going through, and I wanted to help.

'If Sean and Sheila decide they want Edward to be fostered for a while, it will be a special kind of arrangement,' said Julie.

She explained that she'd made it very clear to them that Edward wasn't being taken into care. They would still have full parental responsibility and they could see him or take him home whenever they wanted.

'We've offered them the option of providing somewhere for Edward to live hopefully temporarily,' she said.

'Hopefully temporarily?' I questioned.

'The plan is we'll give Sean and Sheila a break and then at some point we hope that Edward will eventually go back home and live with them and his brother.

'But you know as well as I do, Maggie, that plans sometimes change. It's going to be a huge change and upheaval for the family to care for Edward long term. Sean and Sheila only want what's best for him and I know they're worried that they can't cope. Unfortunately, if that's the case then we may be looking at adoption.

'If you do decide you'd like to foster Edward, then unfortunately I can't give you a time limit or let you know how long you will have him. It could be days, weeks, months. I'm afraid it's just a case of wait and see at this point.'

'What happens now?' I asked.

'I'd like you to go away and think about whether, if it came to it, you'd be willing to take Edward on, and in the meantime I'll chat to Sean and Sheila and explain that they need to make a decision.'

'When's it likely to happen?'

'As soon as possible,' said Julie. 'As far as the hospital's concerned we've done all we can for Edward and he needs to be discharged.'

'OK,' I said. 'I'll be in touch.'

As I drove home, all I could think about was that poor couple. My heart was instinctively saying that I wanted to help them out.

That afternoon Rachel came round and we talked through what Julie and I had discussed.

'It's just tragic,' she said.

'That poor mum,' I sighed. 'I can't even begin to imagine what she's going through. The guilt must be unbearable.'

I wanted to help them but I was uncharacteristically nervous. I'd fostered children with a range of disabilities before, but I hadn't had experience of looking after a child with severe brain damage.

'I'm being overcautious because the parents have been through so much and I want their son to be in the best possible place,' I said. 'What if his heart stops again or, God forbid, he dies when he's with me?'

'I don't think that's likely,' said Rachel. 'I've looked over the doctor's report and the hospital said he doesn't need any medical intervention.'

The signs were all good. Edward wasn't being tube fed or on oxygen any more, he didn't need any medication and scans had shown he didn't have epilepsy.

'By all accounts he's ready to be discharged,' said Rachel. 'And I really do think you could handle this, otherwise I wouldn't have asked you.'

'I'd have to meet Edward first,' I told her.

'Of course,' said Rachel. 'There's a meeting taking place at the hospital tomorrow, so you can speak to the doctors then, and there's a whole care plan being put in place which they can talk you through.'

'OK,' I said. 'If the parents decide that's what they want, then I'm willing to look after him.'

All I could think about was Sean and Sheila. I couldn't even begin to imagine the pain they must be going through. I was doing this for them and in the hope that one day they'd want their son back. But something like this must have shaken them to the core and ripped their lives apart. Would they ever be able to get over the past and be a family again?

TWO

Mummy's Guilt

The following day, I went back to the hospital for a review meeting with Edward's doctors. Julie the hospital social worker had organised it to talk about his care going forward, and Rachel and I had been invited. We all went into one of the family rooms and sat around in a circle.

As I chatted to Rachel, a couple walked in and I knew instantly that they were Edward's parents Sean and Sheila. I guessed they were in their late thirties and they were one of those couples who stood out because she was several inches taller than him. I took one look at Sheila and it was if I could physically see her pain. She was pale and drawn and looked like she hadn't slept for weeks. Her greasy blonde hair was pulled back in a ponytail and she was wearing grubby jeans and a crumpled T-shirt which hung off her thin frame. This was clearly someone who was trapped in their own little bubble of grief and guilt, who was just existing, and didn't care if they'd eaten or were wearing clean clothes.

Sean, who was a short, squat man, clutched her hand. He looked bewildered and exhausted, and I could see the worry etched in his eyes. Here was a man desperately trying to hold it together for the sake of his wife.

'Right then, let's get started,' said Julie.

'Sean and Sheila I'd like to introduce you to Maggie. She's the foster carer who has offered to look after Edward for a while, if that's what you decide.'

'Hello,' I nodded. 'Nice to meet you.'

Sean gave me a weak smile in return but Sheila didn't make eye contact. At the mention of the words 'foster carer' I'd seen her flinch.

'Maggie will be here after the meeting so you can have a chat to her if you want,' Julie told them.

'Thank you,' said Sean.

The meeting began, and a consultant talked about the accident, what had happened to Edward and how he was doing now. He was very matter-of-fact and, as he spoke, tears streamed down Sheila's face. It had been eight weeks, but understandably things were obviously still very raw for her. I suspected that she was in shock. Her pain was palpable and I wanted to run over and give her a big hug.

She wept silently throughout the whole meeting, dabbing her eyes with a crumpled tissue. It must have been so hard for her, sat in a room full of strangers who were discussing her baby and what was going to happen to him.

Sean just looked frightened and helpless. His wife had fallen apart and he didn't know how to handle this and was trying to hold everything together as best he could. Neither of them said anything as Julie talked about them and where they were at.

'Sean has already had a couple of months off work and he has to go back. Relatives will now help look after Edward's twin, Andrew,' she said.

'I've been talking to him and Sheila about the possibility of Edward going into short-term foster care for a little while until they sort out things at home and feel a bit more able to cope with his disabilities.'

The consultant explained that Edward was ready to be discharged in the next couple of days, so a decision about where he was going needed to be made.

'That's something his parents and I will talk about today and a definite plan will be put in place,' said Julie.

After the meeting, Sheila was still visibly upset. I knew it wasn't a good time for us all to talk, so it was a relief when Sean took her out. Julie stayed behind with Rachel and I for a chat.

'As I'm sure you saw for yourself, Sheila's struggling to cope, but ultimately it's up to her and Sean to decide where Edward goes. I've stressed to them that he's not being taken off them and they can see him whenever they want.'

'Have you got any questions?' she asked us.

'Could you explain to Maggie a little bit more about what looking after Edward would involve?' said Rachel.

'Of course,' she said. 'His body is very rigid so a physio will need to come round and do some exercises with him every day and show you how to do them too. Hopefully he'll continue to make good progress with his eating and start taking more solids. Really, it's just a case of keeping him comfortable and trying to stimulate him as best you can.'

'What's his long-term prognosis?' asked Rachel.

'It's too early to say the extent of the brain damage he's suffered,' said Julie. 'The doctors don't know at this point how much he can understand or what learning ability will come back. However, they think it's doubtful that he will ever learn to walk or talk again, and he'll probably be dependent on a wheelchair as he gets older.'

That was the hard thing for everyone. There were no answers when it came to Edward. It was just a case of wait and see.

'Sean and Sheila know they have to make a final decision today, so I'll be in touch as soon as I can,' said Julie.

'If they decide they want him to be fostered then we'll arrange for you to come up and meet Edward straight away.'

Rachel and I walked out of the hospital together.

'What do you think? she asked. 'Have you changed your mind?'

'Not at all,' I said. 'I really want this placement.'

Although I hadn't met Edward yet, I wanted him to come and live with me mainly because I desperately wanted to work with Sheila. I couldn't stop thinking about her and how much she was suffering, and I wanted to try and help her.

'Now you know a bit more, do you think you can cope with Edward's level of disabilities?' asked Rachel.

'I don't know, but I'm going to give it a damn good go,' I said.

'You'll be absolutely fine, Maggie, and you'll have lots of support around you,' Rachel told me.

'Anyway we don't even know it's going happen yet, so there's no use getting my hopes up,' I said.

Nothing was definite, but as I went to bed that night I hoped and prayed that I would have the opportunity to foster Edward.

Luckily, I didn't have long to wait. Rachel rang me first thing the next morning.

'It's happening,' she said. 'Julie's just called me. Sean and Sheila have decided they'd like you to care for Edward when he's discharged.'

'I'm really pleased,' I said. 'I just wanted to have the opportunity to try and help them all.'

'Unfortunately, as you know this is a bit of an unusual case in that there isn't a clear care plan or timeline in place,' she said. 'It could be for a few days, a few weeks or even a few months.

'The initial aim is to give the parents some breathing space. As you saw yesterday, Sheila's emotionally and physically exhausted.'

'I'm absolutely fine with that and I understand they can have open access to Edward whenever they want,' I said.

Julie had asked if I could go up to the hospital and meet Edward later this morning, with a view to the doctors discharging him tomorrow.

'That's great,' I said. 'It's about time I met this miraculous little boy that everyone's been talking about.'

There was a fair bit I had to do at home to get ready for his arrival, but for now all that could wait.

I felt strangely nervous as I drove up to the hospital. My nerves were about seeing Edward and wondering if I really would be able to cope with such a brain-damaged baby.

One of the nurses was waiting for me and she showed me to his room. There was a cot in there and a pull-out chair with a blanket and a pillow on it, which I assumed was where Sheila had been sleeping. I walked over to the cot where Edward was lying.

'Hello, little man,' I said.

He was a beautiful boy with gorgeous blond curly hair. He was so small and delicate and he looked much younger than a year old. His poor little body was all contorted and stiff, and his fists were tightly clenched. He was wriggling about like he couldn't get comfy and his blue eyes rolled around in his head like they were struggling to focus.

I hadn't known Edward before the accident and I could only imagine how heart breaking it was for Sheila to see her son like this. It must be torturous.

'Can he see and hear?' I asked the nurse.

'It's hard to say,' she said. 'Initial tests have shown we think his hearing is OK and we know he can definitely see light and shade.'

I noticed there was a lovely blue, red and white crocheted blanket in his cot and a little blue rabbit.

'Hello, sweetheart, I'm Maggie,' I told him gently. 'You're going to come and live with me for a little while.'

I stroked his cheek and he stopped wriggling as if he was comforted by that, but there were no smiles or any other signs that he knew I was there.

'He's doing so much better than any of us ever expected,' said the nurse. 'He's a little fighter.'

She explained that Edward had been like a newborn baby after the accident, and had had to learn to do everything again.

'He can sit up slightly now if you prop him up, and his sucking and swallowing reflexes are getting stronger,' she said. 'He's drinking his bottle like a trouper and he's started taking a few mouthfuls of pureed food.'

'Can I pick him up?' I asked her.

'Of course you can,' she said. 'He's a lot more robust than he looks.'

Edward was as light as a feather. Even though his body looked rigid, he was all floppy like a newborn and I had to support his head and neck. I cuddled him on the chair and played with his toes and uncurled his stiff little fingers.

'It's been so hard for his mum,' said the nurse. 'She's been here every day. She must be exhausted. But the one thing I've noticed is that she doesn't ever touch him. I've never seen her pick him up or cuddle or kiss him or even talk to him. It's sad,' she sighed.

'Well, hopefully with time that will change,' I said.

I wondered what was stopping Sheila from bonding with her son. I suspected that it was fear – fear perhaps that if she touched him she'd hurt him again, or maybe fear that she didn't or couldn't love him like this? I didn't know. What I did know was that she needed time to grieve for the Edward that she'd lost and learn to love this new version of him. However, she might have to face the fact that maybe she couldn't. Perhaps it was just too painful for her to see him like this, day in day out? Only time would tell.

After a while, Edward started to moan and wriggle around in my arms, so I got up and walked around the room with him. There was an animal mural on the wall, so I talked to him about that and then I showed him the cloud mobile hanging above his cot. I stroked his hand and he seemed to be soothed by the sound of my voice and the physical contact.

Suddenly there was a knock on the door and Julie popped her head round.

'Hi Maggie,' she said. 'Sean and Sheila are here if you'd like a quick word with them?'

A Family for Christmas

I looked through the glass panel in the door and realised they were waiting outside in the corridor. I wondered how long they'd been there. Putting Edward carefully down, I went out to see them.

'We just wanted to say thank you for doing this for us,' said Sean.

'That's no problem,' I said.

'We were watching you with him,' Sheila told me with tears in her eyes. 'And I'm happy that if Edward has to go to someone then he's going to you.'

'I'm glad,' I said. 'I promise I'll take good care of him and you can see him whenever you want.'

They were going in to see Edward so I left them to it, but as I walked away, Sheila called out after me.

'He will wear his own clothes at your house won't he?' she asked.

'Of course,' I said. 'Just give anything you want him to bring to the social worker and she'll pass it on to me.'

Once again I could see the intensity of Sheila's pain. She'd watched me pick up her son, talk to him and cuddle him – all of the things she couldn't bring herself to do. Every time she saw him, the guilt must have been overwhelming and I felt so sad for her.

As I drove home, I went into practical mode and ran through a mental checklist of all the things I needed to do to get the house ready for Edward's arrival. I'd already decided that he was going to sleep in the little box room next to my bedroom. It was painted pale blue with blue gingham curtains, and there was a rocking chair in the corner and a chest of drawers. I got the cot down from the loft and got out some clean bedding and nappies.

I also needed to tell the girls about our new arrival. By the time I picked Lily up from school and brought her home, Louisa was already back.

'I've got something really exciting to tell you both,' I said. 'We've got a new placement coming.'

'Ooh, is it a girl?' said Lily.

'It's a lovely little baby boy called Edward,' I said. 'He's a year old and I'm going to pick him up from the hospital tomorrow.'

'Urgh babies are sooo boring,' sighed Louisa, doing her best stroppy teenager act. I knew she was more interested than she was letting on.

'Anyway why's he in hospital?' she asked.

'He had an accident and he's been very poorly, so I'm going to look after him for a little while for his parents. But they're going to be coming round to see him whenever they want.'

'Is he going to live with us forever?' asked Lily.

'I don't know how long he's going to be with us yet, lovey,' I told her. 'Hopefully just until his mummy feels better and he can go home.'

I didn't even mention the fact that he was brain damaged. They were used to children with disabilities, and it wasn't as if Edward was attached to any tubes or machines that I needed to point out. With all the children that came to stay with us, they just seemed to accept them as they were.

I could see Lily was very excited about having a baby in the house, and she helped me sort out some toys for him. Louisa was at that age where she pretended not to be bothered and there was a lot of huffing and puffing and eye rolling, but I was sure that she'd actually be a great help to me once Edward arrived. She'd been very patient with our previous placement Ruth, who had realty pushed all of us to the limits at times.

The next morning I went to collect him from the hospital.

'Sheila and Sean have already been in to see him and say their goodbyes,' said Julie. 'They left this for you.'

She passed me a large grey suitcase, and explained that she was handing over to a woman named Frances from the local authority who was going to be Edward's long-term social worker. 'She's spent the morning at the hospital with Sean and Sheila and she's going to be calling in on you later at home, just to check that you're happy.' Then she added, 'she seems lovely.'

'OK,' I said. 'Thank you for all your help and I suppose I best get this little man home.'

'Good luck, Maggie,' she said, 'although I don't think you need it. We all know Edward's in safe hands.'

Thankfully Edward seemed fine in the reclining pushchair that I'd bought with me and he was so small he fitted into the baby car seat with plenty of room, although he seemed very unsettled. The car journey was probably overwhelming for him after being in a small hospital room for so long. The poor little thing moaned and wriggled all the way home. When I got back I laid him out on a duvet on the bedroom floor, where he seemed a lot happier.

While he seemed calmer, I took my chance and opened up the suitcase that Sean and Sheila had sent. It was full of the most beautiful, pristine baby clothes, all freshly washed and neatly folded. On the top were the crocheted blanket and the blue bunny that I'd seen at the hospital, along with a note that I assumed was from Sheila.

Please put the rabbit and the blanket in his cot. Thank you.

I'd just finished unpacking his things when the doorbell rang. It was Frances – Edward's new social worker – who had come round to introduce herself. I'd not worked with her before but she seemed very kind and keen to help. She had a friendly face and, although she was very small and dainty, she was one of those people who bubbled over with energy and enthusiasm. It made a nice change to some of the world-weary social workers I often came across.

'How are you getting on?' she said.

'Fine so far,' I told her. 'Edward seemed really uncomfortable in the car but he seems much happier now he can stretch out.'

She told me that Sean and Sheila had got my address and phone number so they'd be in touch.

'They might ring today, depending on how they feel, but they said they'd call you at some point over the next few days to arrange to come round and see Edward,' she said. 'To be honest I think they've gone home to sleep.'

'That's good,' I said. 'Sleep can be a great healer.'

After Frances had gone, a physio arrived to talk me through some exercises to do with Edward. He showed me how to open his hands and put a small ball in his fist to encourage him to grip it, and how to stretch out his arms and legs and straighten his neck and hips.

'Don't be frightened to be firm with him,' he said. 'It will take a bit of practice but you're not hurting him.'

Edward seemed to enjoy the exercises and was very still as the physio got to work.

A Family for Christmas

He'd just left when the girls arrived home from school. They both loved the excitement that surrounded a new placement. They enjoyed getting to know a new child and having lots of different people coming round to the house. It was all a bit of an adventure for them.

Lily was intrigued by Edward. She got the toy basket that she'd help me sort out and showed him everything in it.

'Why doesn't he grab them or put them in his mouth like most babies do?' she asked me.

'Hopefully one day he will,' I said. 'But after his accident he's got to learn to use his hands and legs again, and that takes time.'

Louisa, as I'd hoped, was being really helpful. She understood that he had special needs and she held him up on her lap while I carefully spoon-fed him some baby rice for tea. It was slow and messy, but thankfully he seemed to take it.

I decided not to give him a bath that first night as he'd already been through enough change and upheaval for one day, but I got him into his pyjamas and tucked him into his cot with his patchwork blanket and bunny, just as Sheila had asked in her note.

'Night night, little man,' I said, kissing him gently on the forehead.

I was nervous about how he was going to settle. Like I did with all the children that stayed with me, I left a little night light on and put a CD of classical music on and left it playing quietly. It obviously did the trick, because when I checked on Edward ten minutes later, thankfully he was fast asleep.

I was just coming downstairs when the phone rang.

'Oh hello, Maggie,' said a voice. 'It's Sean here. Edward's dad.'

'Hi Sean,' I said.

He sounded nervous, and I could tell from the hesitant tone of his voice that he didn't want to chit-chat or be on for long.

'We just wondered how Edward was doing?'

'He's absolutely fine,' I said. 'He's taken his milk and some food. I've had him on a play mat and the physio came round and showed me some exercises to do with him. He's fast asleep now.'

'That's good,' he said.

He didn't ask me anything else and he didn't mention coming round. I didn't mention it either, as I didn't want to put any pressure on him and Sheila. I wanted them to see Edward when they felt ready.

Over the next couple of days, Sean phoned every evening at the same time. I didn't want to bombard him with questions, so I just reassured him that Edward was fine and settling in well, which was true. We were slowly getting into a rhythm and I was working out what he liked. I knew he was soothed by white noise and he liked lying on a duvet on the floor or being propped up in the pushchair with pillows, rather than reclining in it.

Edward had been with us three days when Sean phoned as usual that night.

'Sheila and I wondered if we would be able to come round and see him tomorrow?' he asked.

'Of course you can,' I told him. 'You know you're welcome to see him any time you want.'

We arranged for them to come round the following morning after the girls had left for school. I wondered how they would deal with seeing their son again. Not only that, seeing him in someone else's house being looked after by a virtual stranger. There was no doubt it was going to be hard for them, and only time would tell how they would cope with that.

THREE

First Visits

The doorbell rang just after 9 a.m. and I went to answer it with Edward in my arms.

Sean smiled when he saw his son and he immediately reached out to take him. Sheila didn't acknowledge him or say anything, but she looked a little brighter than the last time that I'd seen her at the hospital. She still looked tired but she wasn't weepy.

'Come in,' I said, leading them through to the living room. 'Would you like a cup of tea?'

'Thanks, that would be lovely,' said Sean. 'I can come and help you if you want?'

'No don't you worry,' I told him. 'You two stay here and spend some time with your son.'

I left them in the living room with Edward while I went into the kitchen and dawdled over putting the kettle on. I knew how important it was to give them some time alone with him. For months they'd been surrounded by doctors, nurses and social workers, and there were always people coming and going in a hospital. I also knew how hard it must be for them to see me, a complete stranger, looking after their baby. They didn't know my home or me and it must have felt odd for them, so I wanted them to feel as relaxed and comfortable as possible.

When I finally brought in the tray of tea and biscuits, I noticed Sean was still holding Edward and Sheila was sat on the other side of the room.

'When you've finished your drink would you like to come and see where Edward is sleeping?' I asked her.

'Oh, er, yes,' she said hesitantly. 'If that's OK.'

'Of course it is,' I told her.

I took her upstairs and showed her the bedroom.

'He seems to like me sitting on the chair with him at night and rocking him a bit before bed,' I said. 'And I put some classical music on the CD player, which really seems to soothe him.'

'It's a lovely room,' she sighed.

Sheila walked over to the cot where I'd put the crocheted blanket and the rabbit that she'd sent in the case. When she saw the blanket, she picked it up and instinctively pressed it to her face, breathing in its smell. As she put it back, I noticed her eyes were brimming with tears and she had a look of longing on her face.

'I can tell that blanket has some special memories,' I smiled.

She nodded. 'My mum crocheted each of the twins one when they were born,' she said. 'They've always shared a cot so they've slept with them every night.

'We bought them the rabbits when I was pregnant and a scan showed it was two boys. Andrew has never been bothered about his but Edward always used to take his everywhere with him and snuggle up to it at night. He was always toddling around with it, dragging it by the ears. We were always scared of losing it as we didn't have a replacement.'

87

Her voice cracked with emotion as she remembered how her little boy had been before the accident.

'Sean and I had tried for a baby for so long so when the boys came along we felt so lucky . . .'

Her voice trailed off as she started to sob.

'Are you OK?' I asked.

She nodded and quickly wiped away her tears.

'Thank you for showing me the room,' she said.

I could tell she was embarrassed that she'd broken down in front of me.

'It's a pleasure,' I said.

I walked over to the chest of drawers and pulled one of them out.

'This is where I've put all of Edward's clothes that you sent with him.'

It was important for Sheila to feel like I was listening to her and taking her wishes into account when it came to her son. I wanted her to feel like she still had some control and was involved as much as possible in his life.

'Would you mind choosing some clothes for him to wear tomorrow?' I asked. 'You know his favourites.'

'No, of course not,' she said.

I could see that she felt pleased that she was being useful.

I also wanted her to feel at home and as relaxed as possible at my house. I showed her the changing mat and where I kept the wipes and nappies.

'If you need to change Edward then you can pop up here at any time,' I said. 'Don't feel like you have to ask.

'And if there's anything else you want to bring from home that you think he might like, then feel free.'

'Thank you, Maggie,' she said. 'I really appreciate it.'

I left her to it in the bedroom and went back downstairs.

Sean was still with Edward in the living room. Unlike Sheila, he seemed comfortable with his son and was happy to hold him and interact with him.

'Sheila and I were thinking it might be nice for her to come round every morning to see Edward, if that's OK with you?' he asked.

'Of course,' I said. 'That's fine.'

'Then we both might come round on an evening when I get back from work.'

'You know you can see him whenever you want,' I told him.

I didn't ask either of them how they were or how they were coping. I'd learnt over the years that it wasn't my place to bombard parents with questions. I could listen but I knew it was better to wait and let them open up to me if they wanted.

After an hour had passed, Sean said they had to go.

'I've got to go to work now,' he said. 'And Sheila should get back to Andrew as my mum's looking after him.'

As they left, Sean leant in and gave Edward a kiss. Sheila didn't go near him and she looked like she couldn't wait to get out of the front door.

'See you in the morning,' I said to her.

'Yes,' she told me.

She wouldn't catch my eye on the way out, but as she turned to go I could see tears were running down her face. I felt so helpless. It was awful seeing this woman being eaten away by grief and guilt, but I didn't know yet how to make it better. Or even if I could ever make it better.

*

After that first visit, Sheila came round every morning by herself. She was very quiet, and she was still reluctant to touch Edward and would avoid going near him. I wondered if that was because she was frightened of hurting him, so I started opening the door to her with him in my arms and I'd dance around with him and jig him about just to show her that he wasn't as fragile as perhaps she thought he was.

I tried every trick in the book to encourage physical contact between them. I asked her to give him a bottle or put him down for a nap or go and get him when he woke up, but she always came up with some excuse why she couldn't do it. When I left the room, I'd plonk Edward in her arms but when I came back she'd always put him back down on the blanket.

One morning, I put Edward down on a quilt and tried to get her involved in doing the exercises the physio had showed me how to do. I showed her how to uncurl his fingers and toes and massage his legs.

'Would you like to have a go?' I asked her.

'No, I'm happy for you to do it,' she said. 'I'm going to go and make us a cuppa.'

I'd shown Sean and Sheila where the tea, coffee and the biscuits were, hoping they'd come to feel at home in my house. Now I realised that putting the kettle on was Sheila's default reaction when faced with the prospect of touching her son. It was as if she was scared of being on her own with him.

As the days passed, I learnt that Sheila enjoyed feeling useful and she liked it when I gave her a task to do. Whether that was washing Edward's bottles out or ironing his clothes and putting them away.

I was getting Edward dressed one morning when I remarked that some of his pyjamas were getting a bit small for him.

'Why don't I get him some new ones?' offered Sheila. 'I can go shopping when I leave here today.'

'That would be great,' I said.

When she came back that evening she brought with her three gorgeous pairs of white-and-blue gingham pyjamas with a sailing boat embroidered on the pocket.

These were all gestures that showed me that she cared about her little boy, but her reluctance to touch or interact with Edward still bothered me.

Normally when she came round with Sean in the evenings, I would leave them to have time on their own with him.

One night it was nearing Edward's bedtime.

'You can stay and give him a bath if you'd like?' I suggested.

'That would be great,' said Sean, but one look at Sheila's face told me she thought otherwise.

'Hadn't we better get back?' she said, looking panicked. 'What about Andrew?'

'Come on love,' said Sean gently. 'It will be nice to help get him ready for bed. Andrew will be fine with your mum.'

Sean carried Edward upstairs and laid him on a mat on the bathroom floor while I turned on the taps. As the bath started filling up with water, Sheila lurked in the doorway looking anxious.

'I've got a special mesh sling that he can sit in that keeps him nice and steady in the water,' I told them, 'so he's very supported and safe.'

Soon the bath was ready and Sean undressed Edward and helped me to put him into the mesh seat. As we started to lower him into the water, Sheila suddenly let out a heart-wrenching wail.

'I – I can't do this,' she sobbed before running out of the bathroom.

Sean ran out after her. He came back a few minutes later.

'I'm so sorry about that,' he said. 'She hasn't given him a bath since it happened. She can't bear to see him in the water. It brings it all back and she starts reliving it all in her head.'

I could have kicked myself.

'I'm the one who should be apologising,' I said. 'It's my fault. I didn't think. I just wanted you and Sheila to feel involved in caring for Edward.'

I'd got it horribly wrong and I was annoyed with myself for pushing Sheila into it. Of course she was anxious and on edge about giving him a bath. The last time she'd seen her son in water he was floating face down in their garden pond. I was sure that image was never far from her mind.

I left Sean to finish off Edward's bath while I went to get him a clean vest and nappy from his bedroom. Sheila was there sat on the rocking chair.

'Are you OK?' I asked her.

She nodded, her eyes filling with tears again. She looked drained.

'I'm so sorry,' I said. 'I should never have suggested that you give him a bath. I just didn't think it through properly.'

'It's not just the bath,' she sobbed. 'It's everything. It's just so hard to see him like that, so helpless. A few weeks ago he was sat in the bath, playing toys with his brother. He loved the bubbles and he used to giggle when I put him in the water. Now he's just lying there. I don't know if he can hear me or if he recognises my voice. Do you think he even knows that I'm there? That I'm his mummy?' she asked me.

'I like to think so,' I said. 'The important thing is to keep talking to him, keep cuddling him so he knows your smell.'

Sheila started to cry.

'It all seems pointless somehow. I just don't know if I'm getting through to him.'

'None of us do, I'm afraid, but we'll never know if we don't try,' I said, taking Sheila's hand. 'All we can do is try.'

And she nodded through her tears.

Edward had been with me for a couple of weeks when Frances came round one night for an update.

'How's it all going?' she asked.

'It's going well with Edward,' I said. 'He seems settled and we've got into a good routine. His needs are quite simple. It's Sheila I'm struggling to make any progress with.'

'How's she doing?' said Frances. 'She doesn't give much away when I see her or speak to her on the phone.'

I shrugged.

'Just the same,' I told her. 'She won't pick Edward up or talk to him and she goes out of her way to avoid touching him.'

'Well I hope that will change and she'll start to bond with him,' said Frances.

'So do I,' I sighed. 'But what if it doesn't? What happens then?'

'We'll give Sean and Sheila all the time they need,' said Frances. 'But it's mid-September now and if, by the time Christmas comes, Sheila doesn't seem any further forwards, then perhaps we'll have to start suggesting other options for Edward.

'I'll have had him nearly four months by Christmas,' I said. 'It would be lovely if they could have him home.'

'Sadly they might start to realise by then that adoption is the best thing for all of them,' said Frances.

I knew my role was to support them whatever they decided, however I desperately hoped that that wouldn't happen, that in time they'd want their baby back and they could be a family again. But Frances was right, we had to face facts and look at every eventuality. Maybe the reality was Sheila could never get over her guilt and just couldn't live with seeing her son like this. I desperately prayed that wasn't going to be true. Edward needed his mummy and daddy. They couldn't give up on him, could they?

FOUR

Truths and Triumphs

As I closed the tabs on the disposable nappy, I bent down and blew a raspberry on Edward's tummy.

'There you go, young man,' I smiled. 'All nice and clean.'

It was early October, and Edward had been with us for just over a month. I was a lot more confident with him and he seemed calmer and more settled. He still didn't show any reaction when we talked to him or played with him, and there were still no words or smiles, but I was hopeful that in time that would come.

Sheila was still coming round every morning, but frustratingly I didn't feel like we were any further forward. She still rebuffed any attempt that I made to try and get her to bond with her son.

I hoped that after she'd broken down that night after the bath a couple of weeks ago, she'd open up to me a little bit more about how she was feeling, but she was like a closed book. I knew she was frightened of hurting Edward but I was sure there was something else stopping her from moving forward, something that she wasn't telling me.

'I think we'll have to get this little boy some new clothes,' I told her as I pulled up Edward's cord trousers and noticed how short they were.

'He's had a growth spurt. What would you like me to do with his old stuff that doesn't fit anymore?' I asked.

'I'd like to keep it,' she said.

'Well, at least it means you've got an excuse to go shopping and choose him some new outfits,' I smiled.

I thought Sheila would be pleased as she'd seemed to enjoy getting him the pyjamas a few weeks ago but she looked panicked.

'I'd rather you chose him some things,' she said. 'I don't know what he'd like to wear.'

'He's your little boy,' I said. 'What would *you* like to put him in?'

Sheila looked at Edward lying there on the changing mat and she shook her head.

'That's not my little boy,' she said quietly. 'That's not Edward.'

As soon as the words had left her mouth, I could tell that she was shocked at what she'd said. However, I could see that, at the same time, it was a relief for her to have said them. It was as if it had opened up the floodgates and I listened as Sheila started to talk.

'I'm fed up of people saying I should be grateful that he's still alive. Even Sean says that to me and of course I am, but it's so, so hard. I just want my baby boy back. I want *my* Edward, not this one.'

She started to cry.

'I miss him so much,' she sobbed. 'I miss coming into a room and hearing him say "Mamma". I miss him standing in his cot with his brother first thing on a morning, beaming at me. I miss him toddling around, dragging his rabbit with him, curious about everything.

'But now he's like this and I don't know what to do for him anymore or how to care for him. I'm worried I'm not good enough for him.

'And the worst thing of all is that I let him down. What happened to him happened because of me. I did this to him Maggie. I ruined his life.'

I went over and put my arm around her and she buried her head in my shoulder. I could feel her body shaking as she wept, and all her hurt, anger and grief came tumbling out. I let her have a good cry before I said anything.

'You're bound to feel a huge sense of grief and loss,' I told her. 'And you're absolutely right. This isn't the same Edward, he's a completely different boy.

'However, he's still your son,' I said. 'I know it's hard, but you need to accept that the old Edward has gone and grieve for him, and then try and learn to love the child you've got now.'

'I'm trying,' she said. 'I'm trying so hard, but to be honest Maggie I don't know if I can. And maybe this Edward deserves better than me. Maybe he's be better off with different parents rather than being stuck with a mummy who can't love him.'

She started to cry again and then finally the tears stopped and she looked exhausted.

'Thank you for listening and for not judging me,' she snivelled. 'I know everyone must hate me for what I did.'

'Sheila, nobody hates you and I would never ever judge you,' I said. 'What happened to you and Edward could have happened to any mother. We all make those silly, split second decisions and nine out of ten times it's OK.'

Yes, common sense tells you to never leave your baby unattended by water but so many times in life we make quick judgments and this was one of those judgments that had gone horribly wrong. Sheila was trapped in her own painful world of grief and blame, and I didn't know what to say to her to make it better. There was nothing I could say. All I could hope was that, in time, things would start to change. I wanted to do everything I could to help Sheila bond with her son, but she'd built up this brick wall of guilt, fear and blame that was stopping her from moving forward.

'Throughout all the years I've been fostering, I only have one mantra,' I told her. 'And that's you can't change the past but you can change the future.

'This little boy needs you and I know in my heart that you can give him a wonderful life.'

'I'm scared, Maggie,' said Sheila. 'I don't know how to be around him.'

'Just give it a try,' I said. 'That's all you can do. You owe that to Edward.'

After that I felt that things had finally shifted with Sheila. She was still very nervous around Edward, but she actively tried to be more involved.

A few days earlier I'd got Edward a special foam chair that supported him in a sitting up position and would help to develop his neck muscles. Ever since it had arrived, I'd tried to encourage Sheila to have a go at strapping him into it, but she'd always refused.

'It looks a bit complicated,' she'd told me. 'I'd only get confused. You do it.'

At one point I'd even pretended I'd jarred my back in the hope that she'd do it, but she was still reluctant. But a day after our conversation, she offered to give it a go.

'I'll put him in the chair if you like,' she said.

'That would be wonderful,' I told her.

Her hands were shaking with nerves as she fumbled with the harness that strapped him into it, but eventually she did it.

'Perfect,' I said. 'You've got the knack and he looks very comfy.'

None of us were an expert when it came to looking after Edward, and I was constantly learning too. The doctors and the social workers had advised me to give him as much stimulus as possible and I'd decided to do my own research. I read as many books as I could and talked to other foster carers who had experience of children with cerebral palsy.

Every afternoon, when the physio had gone and we had a spare couple of hours, I'd set up a little experiment. One day I filled a paint tray with sand from the sand pit in the garden and moved Edward's hand in it so he could feel the texture of the grains running through his fingers. The next day I got a handful of ribbons and brushed them over his face.

'Can you feel that, Edward?' I said. 'Is that ticklish?'

The first few times I did it, there was no reaction. But after a while I was sure I noticed him wriggle about a little in his chair.

'Do you like that Edward?' I said, as I brushed the ribbons up and down his legs. I was amazed when he moved his feet up and down.

'Clever boy!' I said. 'You like the feel of them, don't you?'

I did it again and each time he showed the same reaction. The following day I tried running feathers up and down his arms and I clasped his hands around a sandpaper block so he could feel the different textures. He started to react to things, either by wiggling around or moving his arms and legs. It was wonderful to think that he was starting to communicate with us.

Some of my other experiments were slightly less successful. One book I read recommended giving children a bath with oatmeal to soothe their skin and add a bit of texture to the water. I didn't have any oatmeal so I threw in a few handfuls of porridge oats instead. As Edward wallowed in the warm water it became obvious I'd made a mistake and the bath quickly turned into a huge vat of sticky porridge. I added more water but that only made the oats swell up even more and become more glutinous and congealed. It was a total disaster! I had to rinse both Edward and the bath tub down several times to get all the porridge off. Louisa looked at me like I was completely mad and gave me one of her eye rolls.

'I think I'll stick to having porridge at breakfast time,' I told her.

For days afterwards I was still picking bits of dried oats out of Edward's hair!

To be honest I was being a little bit sneaky doing all of these activities in the afternoons when Sheila and Sean weren't there. But I wanted to see for myself what Edward was capable of and then show them what he could do.

When Sheila came round one morning, I plonked Edward into her arms.

'Please could you hold him for a minute as there's a wash I need to sort out?' I asked.

'Yes, of course,' she said.

'Why don't you take him to have a look at the wind chimes hung up by the back door?' I innocently suggested. 'He seems to really like those.'

We went through to the kitchen and while I unloaded the washing machine, Sheila went over to the wind chimes and gave them a little push so they jangled and jingled. Suddenly Edward reached out his little hand and batted them.

Sheila stood there, her mouth hanging open in amazement.

'Maggie,' she gasped, turning to me. 'Did you see that? I'm sure he just reached out to touch the wind chimes.'

It was something that he'd done with me before but I wanted Sheila to see her son's progress and feel like she was discovering it for herself.

'Really?' I said. 'See if he does it again.'

Sheila pushed the chimes and sure enough, Edward reached out again and tried to grab them.

'Look!' she said. 'He definitely did it. Clever boy Edward.'

I could see how proud and pleased she was.

'I can't believe it,' she said. 'That's the first time I've seen him react to something.'

'Like the doctors said, the brain is an amazing thing, and even they weren't sure how much or little it was going to affect his development,' I said.

We all knew that cerebral palsy could never be truly cured, but I think doctors often give the worst case scenario. All the signs were that, little by little, Edward was capable of doing so much more than we thought he was. His movements were jerky and stiff but he was trying so hard to communicate with us.

Buoyed by my recent successes, for my next experiment a few days later I covered Edward with a plastic apron and filled a paint tray with spaghetti hoops. Again it was all about exploring texture so I put his hand into the gloopy mixture and moved it around, helping him squash some of the hoops with his fingers. I could tell he was enjoying it as he started wriggling around with excitement.

'Yuck that looks disgusting,' said Louisa surveying the mess.

'Well, Edward seems to like it,' I said. 'Isn't that right young man?'

I couldn't believe it when he moved his hand up to his mouth and started making smacking noises with his lips.

'Look Maggie he wants to eat them!' shrieked Lily. 'He wants to eat the hoops.'

'I think he does,' I smiled. 'Perhaps he recognises the smell?'

I was so proud of him. The jerky spasms were slowly stopping and he was learning how to control his limbs a bit more.

It was huge progress. Sheila arrived ten minutes later and I couldn't wait to show her.

'I know this is a bit of a strange question but has Edward ever had spaghetti hoops?' I asked her.

'Her certainly has,' she smiled. 'He only recently tried them but they're his absolute favourite.'

'Why do you ask?'

'Come into the kitchen I've got something to show you,' I said.

When we walked into the room, she laughed at the sight of Edward, his apron and hands covered in tomato sauce.

'Do you want me to clean him up?' she said.

'I want you to watch something first,' I told her.

I'd got a clean plastic bowl and filled it with the remainder of the can of spaghetti hoops. I dipped Edward's hand in it and he started making lip-smacking noises.

'He remembers,' grinned Sheila.

'I think he recognises the smell,' I said. 'Do you want to try feeding him some?'

Tentatively Sheila got a spoonful of hoops. Edward opened his mouth like a baby bird and managed to swallow them.

'You remember the hoops?' she said. 'They were your favourites.'

His progress gave Sheila a huge boost. There were other things that I'd started to notice too. One afternoon when Sheila arrived and walked in the room, I was sure that Edward had turned his head towards her. I thought I was probably mistaken so I didn't mention it, but I noticed that it kept on happening.

'He definitely knows you're there,' I said. 'His head instinctively turns towards you when you walk in the room.'

'Do you think so?' she said. 'The doctors weren't sure what he could actually see.'

'I'm positive,' I said. 'I think he recognises your smell.'

Sheila wore a very distinctive flowery perfume and I thought that perhaps was what Edward remembered.

'Well I appreciate you saying it but I think you're imagining it,' said Sheila.

However, one afternoon when Sheila arrived, Edward was propped up in my lap having a bottle and when she walked in the room his head swiftly turned around towards her like a little owl. I looked at Sheila's shocked face and I knew this time she'd seen it.

'I told you,' I said. 'He knows his mummy's here.'

Her eyes filled up with tears.

'He really does, doesn't he?' she said. 'He really knows it's me.'

I could see that understandably this meant the world to her.

'Hello, sweetheart,' she said coming over to him. 'Mummy's here.'

I could see that Sheila was beginning to feel like his mum again and naturally that involved doing things for him. One afternoon she popped round and asked if she could take Edward for a walk.

'Of course you can,' I said.

In the afternoons I'd often take him out for a stroll around the block or to the park with Lily after school. I'd never done it in the mornings with Sheila because she'd never seemed keen. He liked being in the buggy propped up with some cushions.

'I'll just have a quick stroll round the block,' she said.

I watched her walk down the street with him and I smiled. She was really trying. They were gone ages and when she finally came back she was grinning from ear to ear.

'We had a lovely walk,' she said. 'I hope you don't mind but he started to cry so I got him out and we sat on a bench together watching some birds in the fields.'

'Don't be daft,' I said. 'He's your son you can spend as much time together as you want.'

'Thanks,' she said. 'I'd better get back home to Andrew now, but Sean will probably pop round later.'

'OK,' I told her. 'See you tomorrow.'

I was holding Edward in the hall and Sheila was about to open the front door when suddenly she stopped, turned around and walked back towards me. She bent down and gave Edward a kiss on the forehead and stroked his little blond curls. It was just a little peck but that was the first sign of affection that I'd seen her voluntarily give him and to me it spoke volumes. After fearing the worst for so long, I told myself, *Maybe, just maybe, things were going to be OK after all.*

FIVE

Brothers Reunited

Screeches of excitement echoed through the kitchen as I brought out a washing up bowl filled with water and apples.

'Yeah, apple bobbing!' yelled Lily, who was dressed as a skeleton. 'Please can I go first?'

We always make a big deal of Halloween in our house and this year she'd been allowed to invite five friends round for a little party. Even Louisa and I had shown willing and were both sporting a witch's hat for the occasion.

Sean and Sheila had popped round for their usual visit before bedtime and had been drawn into the chaos. I didn't want Edward to miss out on the fun so I'd dressed him in a little pumpkin outfit that I'd picked up at the supermarket.

'Oh, look at him,' laughed Sean when he saw his son.

'I hope you don't mind,' I said. 'I couldn't resist.'

'Not at all! He looks cute, doesn't he Sheila?'

'He really does,' she smiled.

The one thing about six-year-old girls is the noise, but Edward coped really well with the screams and shrieks of excitement.

After apple bobbing and a little treasure hunt I'd set up around the house, I got out some sparklers. I turned all the lights off and opened the back door and the children stood outside while I lit them. Edward, who was sat inside in his chair, was absolutely transfixed as he watched them through the doorway. His little legs kicked with excitement as they waved their sparklers around in circles and spelt out their names.

After the party was over and Lily's friends had all gone home, I started clearing up.

'I'm really sorry it's not the usual organised bedtime routine,' I said. 'We're a bit disorganised tonight.'

'Why don't we stay a bit later to give you a hand?' said Sean. 'Sheila and I can give Edward a bath.'

'Are you sure?' I said, mindful of the disastrous attempt last time when I'd forced Sheila into it.

'We'll be fine,' said Sean. 'Won't we Sheila?'

She nodded, although she looked terrified. 'Like you said, Maggie, I need to give things a try,' she told me.

'OK, thank you,' I said, my heart lifting. I knew what a big deal it was for her, being around Edward in the water.

I started the clean-up operation downstairs while they took Edward upstairs. I didn't want them to feel like I was looking over their shoulder, so I left them to it. Sean knew how to use the harness and how to support Edward in the bath. After twenty minutes I went up to check if they needed anything.

'Is everything OK in there?' I asked.

'Absolutely fine,' said Sean.

I poked my head around the door. Edward was on a changing mat on the floor and Sean was just putting on his pyjamas.

'It looks like you've got everything under control,' I said.

'We certainly have,' he said. 'Sheila did brilliantly.'

She had a big smile on her face.

'We didn't need to use the chair,' she said proudly. 'His neck and back are strong enough now for me to hold him up in a sitting position in the water. He seemed to really enjoy it and he felt nice and secure.'

I knew holding him herself must have given Sheila that extra security too. I could see that she was both delighted and relieved to have done it and to have finally faced her demons.

'I showed him the squeaky ducks and he was kicking his legs around,' she said. 'He seems to really love the water.'

I was so pleased, as I could only imagine how difficult it must be for her to get over that trauma.

I left them to put Edward to bed and eventually they came downstairs and I made us all of a cup of tea.

'Before you go, there's something I wanted to chat to you about,' I said. 'It's something I've been thinking about for a while. I wondered what you thought to the idea of bringing Andrew round to see his brother?

'It's just a suggestion, of course,' I added. 'I just thought Edward might benefit from seeing his twin.'

I didn't want them to feel like they were being pushed into it, and it certainly wasn't my place to make them do something they didn't want to, but I really felt that both twins needed to see each other as they'd been apart for so long.

'We've been talking about that a lot too,' said Sean. 'I think it's a good as time as any, but I know Sheila has her reservations.'

Sheila sighed.

'I don't know,' she said. 'I'm just worried it will upset Andrew to see his brother like this. He's too little to really understand what's happened.'

I knew that wasn't Sheila's biggest fear. She'd already admitted to me that her main worry was that Andrew wouldn't recognise his twin.

'I think it would be good for both of them,' said Sean, looking at Sheila. 'How about we give it a go?'

'OK,' she shrugged.

We arranged for them to bring Andrew with them when they came round the following day. It was a Saturday, which meant that Sean didn't have to rush off to work and everything would be a lot more relaxed.

When they arrived the next morning I could see that they were both anxious. Andrew, who really was the mirror image of Edward, wriggled around in Sean's arms.

'He's gorgeous, just like his brother,' I said, as he gave me a cheeky grin that showed off his two teeth.

'He's just started walking so all he wants to do is tear around,' said Sean.

Although they were identical, I was struck by the stark difference in their physical condition. I could see why having the boys together again would be so painful for Sheila and only accentuate what they'd lost.

As I followed them through to the living room, I could feel their nerves and I started to wonder whether I'd done the right thing in suggesting it.

Edward was lying on a duvet on the floor and I'd put a few toys out around him that I thought Andrew might be interested in.

'Look, Andrew, who's this?' said Sean gently, setting him down on the carpet next to Edward. 'It's your brother Edward. Are you going to say hello?'

Sheila hung back and sat down silently on the settee. I could tell she was on the verge of tears and struggling to keep it together.

'What shall I do?' Sean asked me. 'I don't want Andrew to hurt him.'

'Just leave them be and see what happens,' I said.

He sat down on the sofa next to Sheila and we all waited with baited breath to see how the twins would react to each other.

Andrew didn't seem to notice Edward at first and was more interested in the toys. He toddled over to a musical drum and watched it light up and make a noise when he pressed the buttons. After a while he picked it up, crawled back over to Edward and carefully put the drum down on the floor next to his brother.

'Dah!' he said, patting him gently on the arm.

'Bless him,' said Sheila, her eyes shiny with tears. 'He's giving the toy to Edward.'

'He certainly is,' I smiled.

Over the next half an hour, Andrew explored all the toys in the room and after he'd played with each one, he carefully took it back to the duvet where his brother was lying and gently placed it next to him. Soon Edward was surrounded by a circle of toys.

All that was left on the carpet now was Edward's favourite blue bunny. Andrew picked it up, walked over to Edward and gently placed it on his tummy.

'Bab!' he smiled. 'Bab!'

'That's what he calls his rabbit,' said Sean, who I could see was welling up.

We all watched as Andrew lay down next to Edward, rested his head on his chest and gently stroked the rabbit. I think we were all close to tears as he cuddled up to his identical twin.

'He knows it's him,' said Sheila. 'He knows it's his brother.'

'Of course he does,' said Sean. 'They're identical twins. It's an unbreakable bond.'

Andrew smiled over at us.

'Bab!' he said again, pointing to Edward.

'That's Edward, isn't it?' said Sheila. 'That's your brother.'

Without a doubt Andrew knew that this was his twin, but amazingly at the same time he seemed to know that something was different, that something major had changed. He was extremely careful and loving with him, patting his head and stroking his arm.

'He's not normally this gentle,' said Sean.

Edward seemed very settled and chilled out. He lay there, completely still as Andrew babbled away at him.

'Right then who fancies a cup of tea?' said Sheila, jumping up suddenly. 'I think I'll go and make one.'

Sean was too focussed on the boys to notice, but I knew there was something wrong. After ten minutes I decided to go and check to see if she was alright. I found her sat at the kitchen table staring out of the window.

'Are you OK, Sheila?' I asked.

'I'm just so ashamed of myself,' she sighed. 'I've been shown up by a one-year-old. Andrew knows his brother is different somehow but that doesn't matter to him. He accepted him as he is straight away. Why can't I do that? Why am I struggling? If a one-year-old can do it why can't I?'

'Children are very perceptive,' I said. 'They're often the most accepting. They don't bring all the emotional baggage us adults do to a situation.

'Besides don't be so hard on yourself. You're doing so well. Just enjoy being with your two beautiful boys in there.'

'I know you're right,' she sighed. 'I just feel so guilty all the time.'

It had gone so well that Sheila decided to bring Andrew with her when she came round every morning. Edward, too, seemed to love having his brother there. One morning, Andrew was playing with a spinning top that had mirrors and tiny bells on it. Every child that comes into my house seems to love it as it catches the light and jingles as it goes round. He was sat next to Edward on the floor and, as he spun the top round, Edward suddenly rolled towards him.

'Oh my God!' yelled Sheila. 'Did you see that? He rolled off the duvet towards Andrew.'

She clapped her hands with excitement and pride for her little boy, and Andrew saw her and copied. Sheila laughed.

'That's right Andrew, your brother rolled over to you. Did you see him? What a clever boy!'

She was beaming with happiness.

'You know what, it's so nice to hear you laughing,' I told her. 'I don't think I've ever heard you laugh before.'

It was a wonderful moment and it was lovely to see her enjoying being with her two boys again. I hoped it was the first of many special times that Sheila could share with her sons.

The weeks passed, Halloween quickly turned into Bonfire Night. Edward had been with me almost nine weeks now and had carried on making great progress. Now he was more supple, the physio showed us some more challenging exercises to do to strengthen his muscles. The health visitor was amazed by what he'd achieved and she encouraged us to offer him more finger foods and to try and help him to chew by cupping his chin and gently making a circular motion.

'He needs to relearn the chewing motion again rather than sucking food up,' she said.

The bond between the twins was still there. Both Sheila and I noticed that when Andrew babbled away to him, Edward would blow raspberries and purse his lips and make a 'b-b-b-b' sound.

'Look at him moving his lips,' I said. 'He's trying to talk to him.'

When Sheila would go to take Andrew home, he'd start to wriggle and cry and hold out his arms towards his brother.

'It's OK, Andrew,' Sheila soothed. 'You'll see Edward tomorrow.'

Now she felt able to cope with bath time, Sheila often stayed a bit later on an evening and helped me get Edward ready for bed. She was putting his Babygro on in the bathroom one night when I heard her softly singing to him.

She stopped when I walked in.

'Don't stop because of me,' I said. 'What were you singing?'

'Oh it's nothing really,' she said, obviously embarrassed. 'Before the twins went to sleep I'd always sing them that song 'Hushabye Mountain' from the musical *Chitty Chitty Bang Bang*.'

'I know the one,' I said. 'It's lovely.'

'I've been singing it to Edward in the hope that he'll remember it or help him recognise that it's me, but it's silly really.'

'It's not silly at all,' I said. 'Keep singing it to him. Look at how still he is. He's listening to you and taking it all in.'

'Do you think so?' said Sheila. 'It's so hard to tell.'

Although Edward could roll and reach out for things now, we hadn't heard him laugh or seen him smile, and none of us knew if he could. I still hoped that in time, it would come. As it turned out, I was right. A few nights later, when Sheila was changing his nappy and quietly singing the *Chitty Chitty Bang Bang* song, I noticed that half of his mouth was turned up slightly at the corner.

'Look, I think he's smiling at you,' I said.

'Really?' she said.

It was a bit lop-sided and looked more like a grimace than a smile but I was convinced that's what it was.

'I bet he recognised the song,' I said.

After a few days of practice, and much to Sheila's delight, the lop-sided grimace had turned into a proper lop-sided smile.

The progress kept on coming. One afternoon I got Sheila to sit cross-legged with Edward sat facing her in in her lap. She untied the scarf she was wearing and covered her face with it.

'Peek-a-boo, Edward,' she cooed, whipping it away.

His little arms rose up stiffly with excitement and his legs started wriggling.

'He's enjoying that,' I said.

Sheila did it again and again, and Edward wriggled and kicked with joy. After a few goes, he started to make a funny noise.

'It sounds like he's got a sore throat,' I said.

'Honestly, Maggie, I think he's laughing,' said Sheila, grinning.

The more peekaboo she played, the more throaty giggles Edward made.

'See,' she said.

It was incredible to see him responding to his mum like that and I could see what a boost it gave Sheila.

As we waved goodbye to her and Andrew that day, I felt Edward's weight shifting in my arms. He was leaning towards his mummy and brother.

'I think someone wants to come with you,' I said.

Sheila came over and gave him a kiss.

'Night night, little man, see you tomorrow,' she said. 'I'm so proud of you.'

Some evenings Sheila would stay at home with Andrew, and Sean would come round on his own to see Edward. It was during these times that I started to notice how hard it was for him to say goodnight to his little boy, and he began to linger later and later.

After he'd put Edward to bed one night, I asked if he wanted to stay for a cup of tea. We sat in the kitchen and chatted.

'You find it really hard to say goodbye to him, don't you?' I said.

He nodded.

'To be honest with you, Maggie, I just want my little boy home,' he said. 'I want to be saying goodnight to him at our house. I want to be putting him to bed in his bedroom with his brother every night.

'But I know it's the right thing doing it this way. Sheila's been through so much and I know how important it is to go at her pace. She's still carrying so much guilt about what happened. I was worried at one point that she'd never be able to get over that, that it would destroy her. But little by little, she's getting there.

'I just want us all to be together again under one roof and get on with life as a family.'

'I know you do,' I told him, 'and I'm sure that will happen one day. Just give her time.'

'I must admit there was a time in the beginning when things were so bad that I couldn't see us ever having Edward home with us again,' said Sean. 'When the social worker touched on the idea of adoption, I was adamant that that would never happen, but I could see Sheila was seriously thinking about it. I just couldn't have done it, Maggie. I couldn't have given away our son. I'm just so relieved that things have got better and she feels more of a bond with him now.'

Towards the end of November, Frances came round to see me. She was in regular contact with Sean and Sheila but she liked to check in with me every now and again.

'How are things?' she said. 'I hear Edward's coming on in leaps and bounds.'

'It's going really well,' I said. 'I think the turning point for Sheila was bringing Andrew round and seeing how he reacted to Edward. He immediately accepted him for who he is now, and I think that helped her.

'It wouldn't surprise me if they wanted him back quite soon. It would be lovely if they could have him home in time for Christmas so they could all be together.'

Frances shook her head.

'I did discuss this with them when I went to see them last week. Sheila completely panicked at the suggestion of bringing Edward home.

'She's got to be mentally ready and I'm not sure she's quite there yet. There's still a heck of a lot of guilt there. We've talked about it and even though Sheila knows that Sean doesn't blame her, she has to stop blaming herself. She has to learn to forgive herself.'

Things might not be as straightforward as I had hoped, and the image I'd had of a happy family Christmas in reality wasn't going to happen.

Sean and Sheila were due to take Edward back to the hospital for a check-up with his consultant.

'He's going to be amazed when he sees this little fella,' I said as I waved them off.

But when Sheila brought him back afterwards, I could see that she was in pieces.

'What's wrong?' I asked. 'What on earth did he say?'

'There's nothing wrong,' she said. 'In fact he was really pleased with how Edward was doing.'

Then she burst into tears.

'But that's brilliant,' I said. 'So why are you crying?'

'I'm just being silly,' she said. 'I don't know what I expected. Edward's achieved so much in these past three months, I just assumed it would keep on going. That he would keep on remembering and learning how to do things.'

'And he might,' I said.

'But more than likely he might not,' sighed Sheila. 'I think I just convinced myself that one day he'd be walking and talking and going to school like his brother. I was caught up on wave of hope and optimism. I really thought that we'd got our miracle, but talking to the consultant made me see things a lot more realistically.

'He's always going to be a severely disabled little boy and anything he can achieve is a bonus. But there are no guarantees.

116

I just have to accept that what he can do now might be all he can ever do and that needs to be enough.

'Just ignore me,' she said, wiping away her tears. 'I've got no right to feel like this. I'm just having a bit of a wobble. We've just got to get on with it and look towards the future.'

That was when I knew Frances had been right. On the surface, things had looked like they were going so well, but clearly Sheila wasn't ready yet to take back her son. We were three months down the line and I suppose the main question in my mind was, if she wasn't ready now, then would she ever be? Or, with the clock ticking and the days edging closer and closer to Christmas, did we really have a problem?

SIX

Tinsel and Tears

Wham's 'Last Christmas' blared out from my CD player, and although there were more than three weeks to go, every surface in my house was covered in a light-up snowman, a singing Santa or a talking reindeer.

'Oh I love Christmas,' I sighed, as I put up the last of the decorations.

'I think we can all tell,' teased Louisa, as she stared at the huge tree in the living room that was laden down with baubles and tinsel.

Christmas is my favourite time of the year and I always go to town on decorations and presents, I just can't help myself. The last few weeks had flown by and I couldn't believe it was December already and Edward had been with us for three months. He really felt like part of the family and we all doted on him.

'What do you think then, little man?' I said, holding him up and showing him my efforts.

He managed to focus on the tree and his eyes grew wide with wonder when he saw the lights. His little hand reached out to try and grab a bauble.

'Oh no you don't,' I told him.

'We'll have to show Mummy and Daddy the decorations when they come round later.'

One of them was still coming round every night to help bath him and put him to bed, and I was pleased that Sheila had returned to better spirits. Tonight they both turned up, and they smiled when they saw my handiwork.

'Welcome to Santa's grotto,' I joked.

'Wow, you really do like Christmas,' laughed Sean.

After they'd finished putting Edward to bed they seemed reluctant to go, and I could tell there was something on their minds.

'Is there something you wanted to talk to me about?' I asked them.

'Oh, yes, there is actually,' said Sheila nervously.

'Rather than us coming round here tomorrow, we wondered if it would be OK to take Edward back to our house instead?' said Sean. 'Just for a couple of hours.'

'Of course you can,' I said. 'You don't need my permission, just let me know that it's happening.'

It had always been agreed that they had open access, and Frances had said they could have Edward at their house whenever they wanted, although they'd never done it before now. It was a really positive sign.

The following day Sean came round and picked Edward up.

'How did it go?' I asked, when he dropped him back later on that afternoon.

'It was great Maggie,' he grinned. 'It was so nice to have him at home again and my parents popped in to see him.

'It felt like old times.'

'That's brilliant,' I said. 'And how was Sheila? How did she cope with it all?'

'I think it was good for her. It boosted her confidence and showed her that she can do it. It made her realise that she can look after Edward herself without the security blanket of you always being there in the background.'

'Well, I'm so pleased,' I said.

And I genuinely was. I'd grown to love Edward, his funny throaty giggle and his sheer strength and determination, but I always knew the place he really belonged was at home with his parents and his twin brother.

When Sheila came round the next day I could see that Sean had been right. Edward's visit home really had given her faith in her ability to look after him.

'I was thinking about taking him out to a playgroup today, if that's OK with you?' she said.

'Of course,' I told her. 'Good idea.'

'There's one at the local church that's supposed to be good and I thought it would be nice to take both the boys.'

She paused.

'I'm scared Maggie,' she said. 'What if someone asks me what happened to Edward or why he's like this? What will I say?'

'Just tell them the truth. Say he was in an accident and he's been left with brain damage and cerebral palsy. They don't need to know all the finer details, and if they do start asking questions they're extremely insensitive.'

My heart went out to Sheila. I could see that she was really anxious about it.

'You can't let fear and guilt stop you from having a normal life,' I told her. 'If you pluck up the courage to go then I'm sure you'll enjoy it, and I know the twins will.'

'You're right,' she sighed.

'Do you need to take Edward's pushchair?' I asked her.

'No, it's OK, I've got the double buggy in the boot,' she said.

It was only a little thing but to me that gesture was so telling. It was a sign that Sheila was trying to immerse Edward back into normal life, so that he could join in with his brother again. It was lovely to think of them both sat side by side while Sheila pushed them down the street.

'How did it go?' I asked her when she came back later that morning.

'I'm so pleased you persuaded me to go,' she smiled. 'You were right. No one said anything and the lady who runs it made a big fuss of the twins. It was nice to have someone cooing over the boys again like they used to.'

As I changed and dressed Edward the following morning, I noticed he was continually looking round and his eyes were fixed on the door. I knew exactly what, or should I say who, he was looking for.

'You're waiting for Mummy, aren't you, Edward?' I said.

I lifted him up and gave him a cuddle, and it sounds mad but I could tell from the look on his face that he was thinking, *Thanks Maggie, but I really want my mummy now.*

I was feeding him breakfast in the highchair when the doorbell finally went and he kicked his legs with excitement.

'Here she is,' I smiled.

When Sheila walked in the room a huge grin broke out on his face and his arms reached out towards her.

'There she is,' I smiled. 'There's Mummy.'

She picked him up and gave him a big kiss on his cheeks and he did his throaty giggle. It was wonderful to see.

There was no doubt about it, he knew this was his mummy and finally she knew and loved this version of Edward. It was written all over her face and in her body language when she was around him – the pride in her eyes when she looked at him and the tender way she held him and talked to him. It was all very natural now, nothing was forced or awkward anymore. A mother's love is such a powerful force, and the way Sheila looked at Edward now, you could tell that she would do anything for him. This was her baby boy and there was no way that she was letting him go.

'Come on then, Eddie, where shall we go today?' she asked him.

I'd noticed recently that Sheila had been shortening his name to Eddie, which I'd never heard her do before. I'm no psychologist, but I wondered whether it was her way of moving on and making a fresh start. The old Edward had gone and Eddie was this new boy who she'd slowly grown to love.

'Do you think it would be OK if Eddie stayed at home overnight with us this weekend?' she asked.

'I think that would be fine,' I smiled.

It had already been agreed with Frances that they could do this any time they wanted as long as they let me know.

One night happily turned into two. I could feel that there had been a gradual shift and Sheila was trying to absorb Edward slowly back into normal life. Instead of coming round and staying at home with me the next morning, she took him to visit family. Then, instead of coming back at lunchtime, she took both boys back to their house. Edward was out for most of the day and Sean brought him back just before bedtime and help me put him to bed.

While I was delighted for them that things were coming together so well, if I was being honest I felt at a little bit of a loss. I was now just an early morning and night-time carer for Edward. Not that I didn't relish that. I loved the mornings when I walked into his bedroom and he would greet me with a big lop-sided smile and a giggle.

The following weekend Sheila picked Edward up on Friday morning and Sean dropped him back on Monday morning.

'Things are going brilliantly,' I told Frances when she called round for a chat. 'So brilliantly, in fact, that I feel like a bit of a spare part. Edward's spending most of his time at their house, he may as well be there full time now.'

'You're completely right,' she said. 'But like I've said before, it's got to come from Sean and Sheila. They've got to be the ones to tell us that they're ready and that they want Edward to come home permanently. I think it's a confidence thing. They just need to know that they can do this, that they can cope.'

I knew that they could do it; they just needed to believe it themselves.

'It's not that I want Edward to leave,' I said. 'Far from it. But now we know that adoption is no longer an option, going home is the best thing for him.'

In the three-and-a-half months that I'd had him, I'd grown so attached to Edward. I couldn't help myself. He was a special little boy who had achieved so much despite all the odds being stacked against him. He was always going to face challenges in his life, but he'd shown all of us that he was still there and found his own ways to communicate with us.

Recently he'd learnt how to blow raspberries, which he loved to do mostly when I was feeding him his breakfast. He'd take a big mouthful of porridge, blow a huge raspberry and food would go flying all over the place.

'Oh, Edward,' I'd sigh, and we'd developed a little routine where I would look over the top of my glasses at him and pretend to be cross and he'd copy my eye movements and then dissolve into a fit of giggles. This was lovely, as neither Sheila nor Sean wore glasses so I knew it was a special thing that Edward saved to do for me. Yes, it was impossible not to have become attached to this brave little boy who had defied all the odds. And although it would be hard, I knew the time had come for us to say goodbye.

I also needed to know Sean and Sheila's plans, as Christmas was fast approaching and me and the girls were going away for four days to stay with my brother Robert and his family.

I'd already mentioned it to Frances several weeks ago.

'I'm more than happy to bring Edward with us but I'm not sure how Sean and Sheila would feel about not seeing him for so long, and especially at Christmas,' I'd told her.

'I'll explain the situation to them,' she'd said. 'Then they can decide if they're happy for you to take Edward with you or the other option is we can find a respite carer in the area who can look after Edward while you're away, and then Sean and Sheila can still see him every day as normal.'

Neither of them had mentioned Christmas to me, which was strange as I knew Frances had told them about our plans, but with less than a couple of weeks to go, I knew I needed to talk to them about it and see what they'd decided.

'I wanted to have a chat with you about something,' I told them when they came round the following day. 'The girls and I are going to spend Christmas with my brother. I'm more than happy to take Edward with us, but I just wanted to let you know and see what your thoughts were.

'Well actually, Maggie, Frances has already spoken to us about Christmas and we've been thinking about it and there's something we need to talk to you about too,' said Sean.

He looked at Sheila.

'You've been absolutely amazing,' he said. 'You've looked after our son and picked us up and supported us when we were at our lowest.'

'Edward's been so happy with you and he's made such amazing progress,' smiled Sheila. 'But we think it's time for him to come home. We'd like to him to be back home permanently with his brother so we can have a proper family Christmas. It seems like the perfect time, especially with you going away.'

'I hope you don't mind,' added Sean. 'We're so grateful for all you've done.'

'Of course I don't mind,' I said, completely surprised but delighted. 'That really is wonderful news. I'm thrilled for all four of you.'

It was the news that I'd desperately been hoping for for so long, but it had taken me by surprise as I'd convinced myself that it was never going to happen. I was genuinely so happy for them and as I gave them both a big hug, I found myself welling up. However, there were the practical details to sort out too. You couldn't just hand a child back. For everyone's sake Edward would need to be settled in gradually back at home.

'There's just under two weeks left until Christmas,' I said. 'So we need to speak to Frances ASAP and put a plan in place to transfer Edward's care over to you.'

'Do you think there's enough time?' Sheila asked anxiously.

'I'm sure there is,' I said. 'We all want to make sure that you have him home so you can all be together at Christmas.'

Frances organised a meeting at my house the following week with Sean, Sheila and my social worker Rachel. We talked about how things had gone so far, the times Sheila would be on her own with the boys and what support she had in place.

'Well, you know I will always be here if you need me,' I told them. 'I'd be happy to have Edward for the odd afternoon if you need a break.'

'Thank you, Maggie,' said Sheila. 'That means a lot.'

Sheila also talked about far she'd come.

'It's been hard,' she said. 'When Maggie first met me I was at rock bottom. I didn't think I could hold Eddie, never mind take him home for good. But I know now that's what we want to do.'

The funny thing was, Edward was sat on Sheila's lap throughout the meeting and while she was talking he was patting her face to get her attention and to get her to focus on him.

'Well he certainly knows who his mummy is,' smiled Frances.

What struck me most was how different Sheila was from the person I'd first met more than three months before. She'd been a broken woman who had sobbed her way through that meeting. Thankfully, now things couldn't be more different. She'd put her guilt to one side and was confident now that she could look after him, that they could do this.

'Maggie, as far as you're concerned, do you think Edward can be settled in at home before Christmas?' asked Frances.

'I don't see any reason why not,' I said.

He had already been spending weekends at home, so now he would be going for the odd night in the week too.

'The physio has already been seeing Edward at home in the week,' I said. 'And he doesn't need any medical equipment so to speak of any more.'

His back and neck muscles were strong enough that he could sit up in a highchair now, and he no longer needed the bath sling or the special foam chair.

'Well it looks like we're all in agreement,' said Frances. 'Edward will be home permanently by Christmas Eve.'

Sean looked at Sheila and squeezed her hand. Tears were streaming down her face, but this time they were happy tears.

'I can't wait to have him home,' she smiled.

Over the next few days I started to send more of Edward's clothes and toys home with him when he went for a visit. Sheila already had the double buggy and a car seat. I also knew I needed to tell Lily and Louisa what was happening.

'I've got some great news,' I told them. 'Edward's going to go home to live with his mummy and daddy. Isn't that lovely?'

'Aww,' said Lily, annoyed. 'I wanted him to be at our house at Christmas so I could see what Santa bringed him.'

'Well, Santa's going to be bringing his presents to his mummy and daddy's house instead,' I said.

'Good,' said Louisa. 'Babies make far too much noise. so it will be nice not to be woken up by him on a morning.'

Despite her reaction, I knew both Louisa and Lily were going to miss him. They loved Edward but it wasn't a big shock for them as we'd always said that we hoped he would be going home to live with his parents one day.

On the day before he left, all Edward had at my house was his blanket and fluffy bunny, his bottles and a couple of books.

Sean dropped him off for his final night at my house. We'd agreed that I would do one last bedtime with him. The girls helped me bath him then I read him a story on the rocking chair and savoured every last moment.

'Good night, precious little man,' I told him.

I was surprised when I was woken up at 2 a.m. by a noise from the baby monitor. Edward had always been a great sleeper and had never once woken up in the night before. However, he didn't sound upset; in fact, from what I could hear on the monitor he was babbling to himself, but I decided to check on him just to make sure.

I crept onto the landing and peeped my head around his bedroom door. Too late. His eyes met mine and he gave me a lovely lopsided grin. Normally at that time of night I wouldn't engage with a baby, I'd try and settle them straight back to sleep, but tonight I couldn't resist.

'Come on then, little man,' I said, picking him up.

I sat and cuddled him on the rocking chair, burying my head in his silky blond curls and breathing in his sweet smell. I'd broken all my own rules and I knew this was more about my need than Edward's; however, he seemed very contented and happy as he nestled into the crook of my neck.

'You're going home in the morning, Edward,' I whispered. 'You're going home to your mummy, daddy and your brother Andrew and you're going to have the most wonderful life. Just you wait and see.'

I gently kissed his forehead and put him back down in the cot, tucking his favourite blue bunny under his arm. As I walked out of the bedroom, I felt a familiar heavy sadness in my heart, as I knew that that had been our goodbye.

The next morning, we woke up to one of those perfect winter days. The sun was shining and there was bright blue sky, but it was bitterly cold. We were up early as Sean and Sheila were coming first thing to collect Edward. As we had breakfast, I could see the frosty grass in the garden sparkling in the sunlight.

'It looks all twinkly like diamonds,' said Lily.

'It does a bit,' I said, spooning porridge into Edward's mouth that was open like a baby bird. 'It would be great if it snowed, wouldn't it? We haven't had a white Christmas in years.'

I was just loading the breakfast things into the dishwasher when Sean and Sheila arrived. I always like to keep goodbyes short and sweet, as I think that's better for everyone. This goodbye in particular was very positive and it was the happy ending that we'd all hoped for. However, no matter how many times I'd done it over the years, letting go of a child never got any easier.

Sheila strapped Edward in the car seat in the hall as Louisa, Lily and I waited to wave them off.

'I hope you don't mind but we got the girls a little Christmas present,' said Sean.

'Thank you,' said Louisa and Lily in unison as he handed them two beautifully wrapped boxes.

'And we got a little something for the twins,' I smiled, handing him two packages that contained a wooden train with Andrew and Edward's names on them.

Then Sheila turned to me.

'Eddie and Andrew have made you a special Christmas card,' she said, handing me a card with their little hand and footprints on.

'It's gorgeous,' I said. 'I'll treasure it.'

Despite my best efforts at not having an emotional goodbye, there was something about seeing those little footprints that brought tears to my eyes.

Don't cry Maggie, I told myself, *it's not helpful for anyone.*

They'd also got me a lovely poinsettia plant.

'Maggie I don't know what to say to you,' said Sheila. 'Thank you just doesn't seem to be enough. You got me through the most horrendous time of our lives and . . .'

Her voice was so choked up with emotion she struggled to go on, and I felt myself welling up again.

'You don't need to say anything,' I told her, stroking her arm. 'It's been an absolute privilege to get to know you and your little boy. Now, you go home and enjoy Christmas with your two beautiful sons.'

'Don't worry we will,' said Sean. 'Thank you for everything.'

'You know where I am if you need me,' I told them, tucking Edward's favourite blanket over him to keep him snug in the car seat.

'It's bitter out there,' I said. 'Drive carefully.'

I could see they were itching to get home where they had family waiting with Andrew for them.

'Merry Christmas!' shouted Sean, as he wound down the window.

Sheila, who was sat in the back seat with Edward, waved as they drove away. She looked so happy.

'Right then, girls,' I said, swallowing the lump in my throat as I closed the front door. 'We'd better get packing as we've got to set off tomorrow.'

I knew I'd have a little cry later, when Lily and Louisa went to bed, as I didn't want to upset them. It was good to have the excitement of Christmas to take my mind off the fact that Edward had gone, and I was pleased that we were going away. The house was full of painful reminders – coming across a nappy and some wipes in my handbag, or finding a toy he'd liked on the floor or wandering into his bedroom that still smelt of him. Why was saying goodbye always so hard?

The following day, with the car packed to the gills with presents and food, we set off for my brother's house. On Christmas Day, as I tucked into turkey with all the trimmings, I couldn't help but think of Sean and Sheila, sat around the table with their two boys and enjoying being a family again at long last.

'I'd like to make a toast,' I said, although everyone looked at me like I was mad.

'To Edward, the bravest little boy I know,' I said, raising my glass.

'To Edward!' said everyone.

And finally I knew in my heart that things were going to be just fine.

Epilogue

When Sean and Sheila left, I told them that they knew where I was if they wanted me.

'We'll be in touch and come and visit,' Sheila told me, but I knew in my heart that they wouldn't. It was a time of their lives that understandably I think they wanted to forget, and I had to respect that. They'd lived every parent's worst nightmare and now they wanted to start afresh and get on with their lives. As a foster carer you also have to think of what's best for the child. Edward had been with me for less than four months, and as time passed he wouldn't remember me or being at my house.

Six months later, I was fostering a toddler when I bumped into Sheila and the twins at a local playgroup. It was like bumping into an old friend, and it was lovely to see her. Much to my delight, Edward was bum shuffling across the floor and had started to pull himself up on furniture. He gave me a big smile and let me give him a brief cuddle before he wriggled off my lap and back to his mummy.

Sheila promised me that she'd keep in touch and she kept to her word. Every year she sends me a Christmas card with a few lines about how they are all doing. A few months after I'd met her, they moved out of the area and a year later they went on to have another son.

As for Edward, I couldn't be more proud of how well he's done. Over the years, with the help of speech therapy, he regained some limited speech, and he learnt to use an electric wheelchair. He went to a school for children with learning difficulties and is apparently a very talented sculptor. He's just celebrated his eighteenth birthday and is about to go to a residential college for people with disabilities.

I don't think Sheila will ever truly be able to forgive herself about what happened to her son that day in the garden. Her guilt will never totally go, but as the years have passed she has learnt to live with it. I feel very privileged to have helped them through that horrendous time in their lives, and it was wonderful to see them come out of the other side and be a family again.

The Girl No One Wanted

ONE

Late-Night Mission

As I spread out the picnic rug, Louisa started getting our food out of the cool box.

'Maggie, this is all very nice but do I have to stay long?' she asked. 'I said I'd go round to Charlie's later.'

'It's only a picnic, love,' I told her. 'I thought you'd enjoy coming along and seeing Vicky and some of the other foster carers you know. You can go to Charlie's afterwards.'

Every few months my fostering agency put on a social event so carers could all get together. There was always a big party at Christmas and Halloween and now, in the spring, they organised a picnic in the park. I'd just finished a couple of respite placements and, unusually, I didn't have any children living with me at the minute so I'd persuaded Louisa to come along to keep me company. But, like most teens in love, she was much keener to spend time with her new boyfriend than come to a picnic with old me. I opened a bag of crisps and started tucking into a ham sandwich.

'Hi, ladies,' said a voice and I looked up to see Becky – my supervising social worker from the fostering agency I worked for. 'Are you having fun?'

'Well *I* am,' I told her, grinning. 'Madam over here seems more eager to go and meet her new boyfriend.'

Louisa rolled her eyes at me.

'I'm only teasing,' I said.

Louisa had been with me since her parents had been killed in a car crash six years ago. She was about to turn nineteen and even though she wasn't in the care system any more she knew she could live with me as long as she wanted. She'd been with me for so long, she was like my daughter. As a nanny, she was also a great help with my fostering placements and a brilliant support to me as a single foster carer.

'If I buy you an ice cream would that cheer you up?' I said, handing her a couple of pounds.

'Thanks,' she smiled.

She might have been nineteen but a Mr Whippy with a chocolate flake in it was still a favourite of hers.

I watched Louisa stride confidently across the grass to the ice cream van – so different to the scared, timid girl who had turned up on my doorstep with a social worker all those years ago. She was so tall, and her willowy frame was shown off by the high-waisted jeans and cropped T-shirt she was wearing.

I was lost in thought when Becky sat down next to me on the rug.

'Just quickly before I go and mingle, remember the new buddy system we talked about at the meeting the other week?' she asked.

I nodded.

'Well remind me later on to introduce you to Trudy,' she said. 'I thought I might partner you up with her. She's a fairly new foster carer and I think her latest placement is proving quite challenging. Like you, she's a single foster carer so it would be useful for her to have someone to bounce ideas off.'

'Of course,' I said. 'I'm more than happy to help if I can.'

The idea of the buddy system was to partner up a more experienced foster carer with a newer one so we could swap tips and advice.

'I'm not sure I've got all the answers,' I said. 'But I'm happy to have a chat with her.'

'Thanks,' said Becky, getting up. 'I've told her about you and she seemed keen to meet you.

'In fact . . .' she said as she stood up. 'She's sitting over there.'

She gestured to a short blonde woman in her forties.

'The girl with her is her placement Leanne. She's just turned eleven and she's proving to be a bit of a handful.'

'OK,' I said. 'I'll wander over later and say hello.'

'Thanks, Maggie, I appreciate it.' Becky smiled as she left to go and chat to the other families.

I looked across the grass to where Trudy and Leanne were sitting. Leanne certainly didn't look like a handful. In fact she looked very sweet. She was a petite little thing with brown curls and pale skin and was sitting quietly next to Trudy on a picnic rug, watching the other children play.

Louisa came back with her ice cream while I tucked into my picnic and chatted to my friend Vicky, who was sitting next to us with the two sisters she was fostering – three-year-old Teegan and Janie, five.

Fifteen minutes later I heard a real commotion coming from the other side of the grass. People were turning round to look.

'Blimey, that girl's kicking off,' said Louisa.

I looked over and realised it was Leanne – the girl that Trudy, the carer that Becky wanted to buddy me up with, was fostering. She was looking decidedly embarrassed as Leanne began to shout at her.

'I ain't eating that,' she screamed, kicking the cool box. 'Why didn't you bring any food that I liked, you silly bitch?'

It was colourful language for an eleven-year-old but I'm sure most of us foster carers had heard much worse. Trudy, however, didn't seem to be handling it well.

'Sit down, Leanne,' she hissed, her cheeks flushed with embarrassment.

'I ain't siting down,' roared Leanne with a defiant look on her face. 'Not until you get me something that's not crap.'

She kicked the sandwiches from the blanket and flung away the carton of apple juice Trudy had given her.

'Leanne, I said sit down right now,' said Trudy, sounding more and more upset.

But Leanne ignored her and I could see Trudy wasn't going to be able to calm her down.

'I'm going to go over,' I said.

'Are you sure that's not going to make it worse?' asked Vicky.

'I wouldn't normally intervene when someone's child is kicking off but I think a distraction might help,' I replied.

I wandered over to where they were sitting. Leanne was still shouting and swearing at Trudy.

'Oh, hello,' I said, ignoring Leanne. 'You must be Trudy. I'm Maggie. We've got the same supervising social worker, Becky. She thought it would be nice for us to meet up for a coffee sometime so I thought I'd come over and introduce myself and give you my number.'

'Oh, er, yes,' said Trudy, clearly a little confused, and embarrassed about the kerfuffle Leanne was causing. 'That would be great.'

Thankfully me coming over had stopped Leanne in her tracks and she was now stood there staring at me, her arms crossed defiantly.

'And you must be Leanne,' I said in an overly cheerful voice. 'It's lovely to meet you. I was going to invite you and Trudy to come round to my house one day if you'd like that?'

Leanne didn't say a word, she just scowled at me. But at least she was quiet.

I quickly fished a pen and a piece of scrap paper out of my bag and scribbled my number on it.

'Give me a ring anytime,' I said, handing it to Trudy. 'I'm happy to have a chat.'

'OK,' she said, putting it in the pocket of her jeans. 'That would be great. Thanks so much, Maggie.'

She gave me a grateful smile and I could see how much she appreciated the gesture.

Thankfully my interruption seemed to have diffused the situation and for now Leanne was sitting quietly on the grass sullenly watching me.

'Poor woman,' sighed Vicky as I went back over to her. 'That girl seems like a handful.'

'We've all been there,' I said. 'It's hard to know how to handle such a challenging child, especially when you haven't been fostering for long.'

I really sympathised with her. Fostering was never easy or straightforward, no matter how long you'd been doing it; we were all constantly learning. There wasn't a right or a wrong way to do things, all you could do was the best you could for each child.

After a few tricky placements, I'd recently made the decision to focus on mother and baby placements for a while. They were challenging in a different way from a troubled teen or a traumatised child, but I was looking forward to getting stuck in when I got my next placement.

Thankfully the rest of the afternoon passed without any more drama, but after Leanne's outburst Trudy didn't hang around for long. I noticed her packing up not long after I'd gone to speak with her and she gave me a weak smile as she walked off with a sulky-looking Leanne.

'Nice to meet you,' I called. 'Give me a ring.'

She nodded.

Soon I decided to call it a day too. Louisa was going to her boyfriend's for the night so I said goodbye to Vicky and headed off. I was looking forward to a nice relaxing evening on the sofa with a bar of Dairy Milk and a good film.

However, just after 10 p.m. my mobile rang. It was a number I didn't recognise and I felt that little pang of worry you get when you receive a call late at night. I hoped Louisa was OK.

'Maggie?' said a woman's voice on the other end of the line. 'Please can you help me?'

I could barely make out what she was saying, or even who was speaking, she sounded so frantic and upset.

'She's out of control. I don't know how to calm her down. She's smashing up the house and she started hitting me. I'm so scared. Please, please come and help.'

'I'm really sorry, but who is this?' I asked, confused. 'I don't recognise your number.'

'It's Trudy,' said the voice. 'I met you today at the picnic. We're with the same fostering agency. Oh, Maggie, please help me. I don't know what to do.'

She sounded hysterical.

'Trudy, it's OK,' I said. 'Take a deep breath and tell me what's wrong.'

'It's Leanne,' she gabbled. 'She's really angry. All I did was ask her to tidy her room and she just exploded. I was so scared I've had to lock myself in the downstairs loo.'

I could tell that Trudy was incredibly upset but I was also worried about Leanne too and whether she might hurt herself in her rage. I knew this was serious enough that it needed to be dealt with through official channels.

'Have you called the agency and told them what's happening?' I asked.

'I couldn't,' she said. 'My mobile's in the kitchen. I managed to grab the house phone from the hallway and the only number I had was yours on the piece of paper in my jeans pocket.'

She was crying now and I could hear the desperation in her voice. Thoughts raced through my head as I tried to work out what was best to do.

'I'm so sorry for bothering you,' she sobbed. 'I've tried to help her, I really have, but she's pushed me to the limits and she's really scared me this time.'

'It's OK, Trudy,' I said, trying to calm her down. 'Do you want me to ring the agency and tell them what's happened? Then I can get a duty worker to call you back on the home phone.'

'Oh, yes please,' she gulped 'Thanks, Maggie.'

'You stay where you are and I'll get someone to call you straight back. Do you know where Leanne is now?'

'Yes, she's banging on the toilet door and shouting at me.'

I was relieved in a way, as at least I knew Leanne was still in the house and safe.

As soon as Trudy had hung up, I phoned the out-of-hours number for the agency and explained what had happened to the duty social worker.

'I know it's not my place to get involved in another carer's business but she rang me and she's getting quite hysterical. She's locked herself in the loo.'

'Right, OK, thanks for passing that on, Maggie,' said the duty worker, Sarah. 'I'll give her a ring straight back.'

'Thanks,' I said. 'I'd really appreciate it if you could let me know what's happening, just to put my mind at rest.'

'I will do,' said Sarah.

I knew I wouldn't be able to concentrate on a film or go to bed tonight until I knew that both Trudy and Leanne were OK.

I was in the kitchen making a cup of tea when my mobile rang again. It was Sarah at the agency.

'I've spoken to Trudy and she doesn't feel like she's able to diffuse the situation herself,' she said. 'I tried to get her to put Leanne on the phone but she wasn't willing to unlock the toilet door. So I'm going to head over there now and see if I can help. I'm over the other side of town so I should be there in about forty-five minutes.'

'Well I'm only a five-minute drive away,' I said. 'I could be there a lot quicker. Why don't I go?'

'But there's a possible risk of violence, Maggie,' she said. 'I can't risk sending you.'

'I'll be fine,' I said. 'She's a petite eleven-year-old girl not a strapping six-foot teenager. If I really think things have got that much out of control then I'll call you and the police straight away.'

'OK,' replied Sarah. 'As long as you're sure.'

'I'm sure,' I said.

'Then I'll give Trudy a ring back now and let her know. Thanks ever so much, Maggie. Please ring me straight back if you think the situation is out of hand or you need extra help and I'll get straight in the car.'

'I'm sure I'll be fine,' I said.

I'm a firm believer that when a child is kicking off badly, the more people that are involved, the more attention it gives them and they will ramp up their behaviour and turn it into even more of a drama. Leanne's anger was towards Trudy and not me so I felt confident I could deal with the situation and try and calm things down.

'Do you want me to see whether I can get Leanne to come back and stay with me for the night?' I asked Sarah.

'If you're happy to do that and you think it might help, then yes, that's fine,' she said. 'Keep in touch and let me know what's happening.'

'OK,' I said.

I quickly ran upstairs, got changed out of my pyjamas and pulled on some jeans and a top. As I hunted for my car keys, I gave Trudy a quick call.

'Trudy, it's Maggie,' I said. 'Just wanted to let you know I'm on my way round.'

'Oh, thank you so much, Maggie,' she said, clearly relieved. 'Sarah phoned me and told me. I'm so glad you're coming. Leanne's still ranting and raving.'

'Is there any way I can get in the house or shall I knock?' I asked.

'No, don't knock, Leanne won't let you in,' she said. 'If you go to the back door, there's a spare key under the mat. I know it's not very security conscious but I'm always locking myself out.'

'No problem,' I said. 'I'll be round as quick as I can. I don't think I'm far from you.'

'Thank you so much, Maggie,' she said, sounding grateful.

Ten minutes later I pulled up outside Trudy's house – a smart semi-detached in a quiet street. The living room curtains were open and there was a lamp glowing in the front window. It looked cosy and inviting and there was no sense of the chaos that was waiting for me inside. I walked around the side and found the key under the mat. It felt strange letting myself into someone else's house.

'Hello,' I called, as I walked into the kitchen. 'Is there anybody there?'

I looked into the hallway where Leanne was pacing up and down outside the downstairs toilet. Her blue eyes were wide with shock when she saw me and I didn't want to frighten her. 'Hi, Leanne,' I said. 'I'm Maggie. Remember me from the picnic at the park today? I'm the foster carer who came over to say hello to you.'

'What are you doing here?' she snapped, her expression quickly changing to a scowl.

'Oh, I've just popped round to have a cup of tea with Trudy,' I said casually, not wanting to inflame the situation even more by telling her Trudy had called me asking for help.

Unsurprisingly, Leanne looked at me as though I was mad, clearly wondering what on earth this strange lady was doing coming round at this time of night to have a cup of tea.

'Could you come and show me where the kettle is?' I asked her. 'If Trudy's in the toilet let's leave her in peace while you and I go into the kitchen and make some tea.'

My talking was enough to distract her and Leanne followed me into the kitchen and pointed to the kettle on the side. She watched in stunned silence as I filled it with water and flicked it on.

'I bet you know what I'm going to ask next,' I smiled. 'Where does Trudy keep her tea bags and cups? It's really funny when you go into someone else's house and you don't know where anything is.'

Leanne obediently opened the cupboard and showed me the mugs and the biscuit tin full of tea bags.

'Would you like one, or perhaps some warm milk?' I asked.

Leanne shook her head.

I chattered away while Leanne stared at me. I was hoping that Trudy would have heard that I was there and, sure enough, a few seconds later I heard the lock on the toilet door click open. An apprehensive-looking Trudy walked into the kitchen. Her face was puffy and mascara was smeared down her cheeks from where she'd been crying.

I purposefully turned my back to Leanne to face Trudy so I could shield Trudy from her if she started kicking off again. But I think Leanne was still so confused by my sudden arrival that she was quiet.

'Oh, hi, Trudy,' I said casually. 'I've just made us a cup of tea. Shall we go into the front room and have a quick chat?'

I turned to Leanne, who was scowling at Trudy.

'Would that be all right with you, Leanne? We won't be long.'

She shrugged.

Trudy followed me nervously into the front room.

'How are you doing?' I said.

She looked exhausted.

'I feel so stupid,' she said. 'She seems fine now but I was genuinely scared. Things escalated so quickly after I asked her to tidy up. She was so angry, Maggie, shouting and throwing things at me. I didn't know what to do.'

'It's OK, Trudy, don't beat yourself up,' I said, seeing that Trudy was close to tears again. 'We've all been there and it's tough. You did the right thing asking for help.'

'I know she's quiet now but I don't want to be on my own with her,' she sobbed. I reached over to comfort her.

'Do you want me to ask Leanne if she'll come and stay overnight with me to give you a break and a chance to calm down?'

She nodded, breaking into a fresh bout of tears.

'Honestly, things will feel better in the morning,' I told her. I left a tearful Trudy in the living room while I went to see Leanne in the kitchen.

'I was talking to Trudy and she said you'd both been a bit upset so I wondered if you fancied staying at my house tonight to give you a bit of a break?'

She looked surprised.

'Suppose so,' she said.

'I tell you what, why don't you go upstairs really quickly and pack your nightie and your toothbrush then I'll ask Trudy if it's OK.'

I made out like it was a secret plan between the two of us and nothing to do with Trudy. Leanne stomped sulkily up the stairs while I went back to see Trudy.

'I'll take her back to mine overnight,' I told her. 'She seems OK about coming and she's calmed down. If you could give the duty agency worker a ring and let her know, that would be brilliant. Then we'll talk more tomorrow.'

'Thank you so much, Maggie. I'm so sorry for dragging you out,' she said, dabbing her eyes with a soggy tissue but looking relieved.

'Listen, it's no problem at all,' I said. 'I'm happy to help and there's no need to apologise. Have a bath and a good night's sleep and things will feel better in the morning.'

I could see she was still very shaken up about what had happened.

'You stay here and put your feet up and Leanne and I will see ourselves out. Remember, you can give me a ring later if you want to. And you will give Sarah a ring and let her know that Leanne's with me?'

She nodded.

Leanne had packed a rucksack and was waiting for me in the kitchen.

'Let's go then,' I said.

She hardly said a word on the drive back to my place. Thankfully I had one of my rooms already made up with clean sheets on the bed so I put her in there.

'It's straight to bed because it's so late,' I said.

She was quiet and a bit sheepish. I think she realised that she'd overstepped the mark.

'It was all her fault,' she said as I popped my head round the door to say goodnight. 'She's a cow and she's always telling me what to do.'

'Let's not talk about it now,' I said, interrupting. 'I'm very tired and you must be too.'

I wasn't going to get into a row just before midnight. I went downstairs and flopped onto the sofa. But after all that had happened suddenly I didn't feel like watching a film any more. Instead I went to bed with a heavy heart, wondering what new dramas tomorrow would bring.

TWO

Another Move

The next morning I made sure I was up and downstairs well before Leanne woke up. I was mindful of the fact that it would be strange for her waking in an unfamiliar house with someone she hardly knew. Plus she might feel frightened and upset after all the drama that had gone on the night before.

I knew she was awake because I heard her stomping down the stairs. I'd put some boxes of cereal on the kitchen table for her so she could choose which one she liked.

'I hate all of these,' she moaned, pushing them away.

'I'm afraid that's all there is,' I said, pouring her out a beaker of orange juice.

'And I don't like juice,' she said.

I ignored her and carried on.

'Well would you like some toast then instead?' I asked.

'Don't like toast,' she snapped.

Every single thing was a battle and it gave me a glimpse of how she must have worn Trudy down. There was even something wrong with my toothpaste when she went upstairs to clean her teeth.

'I'm not allowed this toothpaste,' said Leanne, storming out of the bathroom. 'I can't have it, I'm allergic to it. It's too minty.'

I'd never heard of a child being allergic to toothpaste before and I didn't quite believe her, but I didn't want to take the risk.

'I've got some strawberry-flavoured toddler toothpaste in the bathroom cabinet,' I said. 'Would that be better?'

'Suppose,' she shrugged.

I'd just handed it to her when the doorbell rang.

'I'm going to answer that but when I come back up I expect you to have brushed your teeth and washed your face,' I said.

I knew it would probably be Trudy as I'd arranged for her to come round first thing to drop off Leanne's school uniform. She looked nervous as I opened the front door to her.

'Where's Leanne?' she asked.

'It's OK,' I told her, leading her through to the kitchen. 'She's upstairs. How are you feeling today?'

She shrugged.

'Still a bit shaken up to be honest,' she said. 'She really frightened me, Maggie. I genuinely didn't know what to do.'

Her eyes started filling up with tears again. I put my hand on her arm as I could see she was still very upset.

'Is that her school uniform?' I said, gesturing to the carrier bag in her hand.

'Oh, yes,' she said, composing herself. 'I've arranged for the taxi that takes her to school to pick her up from here instead of my house.'

Just then the kitchen door swung open and Leanne stomped in.

'What's that cow doing here?' she shouted as she saw Trudy. 'You never said she was coming. I don't want to see her.'

From Trudy's body language I could see she was genuinely intimidated by Leanne. She was literally trembling with fear. It was incredible that this little girl had so much power over her.

'Leanne, this is my house and I choose who I want to come round here,' I told her firmly. 'Now you go back upstairs and get yourself ready for school.'

'But I—'

'But nothing,' I interrupted. 'It's important that I talk to Trudy. Here's your school uniform,' I said, handing her the carrier bag. 'So please, go back upstairs and get ready.'

She snatched it from me and stormed out.

Trudy was in tears again and looked like a broken woman.

'I can see that she's a challenge,' I said.

'That's an understatement,' she replied. 'Every day, every little thing is a constant battle. I know it's my fault. She'd been through so much and naively I thought that by giving her love and security I could help. I can see now I shouldn't have given into her so easily. All she's done is trample all over me.'

'I'm sure you've done all you can,' I told her. 'Fostering is hard. Becky at the agency can maybe try and give you some extra help and advice and some strategies that might work with Leanne.'

Trudy shook her head and the tears started to flow.

'I can't do it, Maggie,' she sobbed. 'I feel terrible, but for my own sanity I can't have her back in my house any more.'

I was surprised at how certain she seemed.

'You have to do what's right for you but don't make any drastic decisions,' I said. 'Talk it through with Becky this morning and tell her how you feel.'

'I will do,' she said, turning to leave. 'But I don't think anything is going to make me change my mind.'

'You take care of yourself,' I told her, following her to the front door. 'I'd better go and check on Leanne.'

'OK,' she said, giving me a weak smile. 'Thank you, Maggie.'

I went upstairs with a heavy heart thinking what a difficult situation this had turned out to be. It was always sad for both the carer and the child when a placement broke down.

Leanne was still in her pyjamas and had ignored my request to get into her school uniform.

'Is she still here?' she glowered.

'No, Trudy's gone now,' I told her.

'I bet she doesn't want me any more does she?' she asked. 'Well that's fine if she's getting rid of me 'cause I hated it at her house. She's a bitch.'

'Leanne, nothing has been decided yet,' I said. 'I know you're upset but you need to get ready for school as the taxi will be here in a minute.'

'I'm not upset,' she snapped. 'She can get rid of me if she wants. I don't care.'

Leanne was only eleven and in her final year at primary school, but she had the behaviour and attitude of a teenager. I could see that she used noise to intimidate and try to control people and it had certainly worked with poor Trudy. I knew I'd done all I could to help with a difficult situation and it was a relief when I managed to get Leanne into the taxi and off to school.

As soon as she'd gone I phoned my link worker, Becky, to fill her in.

'Blimey, you had a busy night,' she said. 'The duty social worker was just filling me in about what had happened with Leanne.'

'Trudy was at her wits' end and in no fit state to be on her own with Leanne, so I thought it was best that I bring her back here,' I said.

'You did the right thing,' Becky replied. 'I'm about to call Leanne's social worker, Jenny, now and then I'll get in touch with Trudy and see what's what.'

'Good luck,' I said. 'She still seemed very raw this morning.'

I put the phone down and got on with some cleaning as well as changing the sheets on the bed Leanne had slept in so it was ready for whoever came next. Becky seemed to think that a mother and baby placement was imminent as she knew a vulnerable young mother who was about to give birth, so I was hopeful my bedroom would be occupied soon.

A couple of hours later I was about to go out to the super-market when my phone rang. It was Becky again.

'Maggie, I've got a favour to ask you,' she said. 'Do you think you might be able to keep Leanne for another three or four nights?'

'That should be OK,' I said, my heart sinking. 'Why, what's happened?'

'Jenny and I went to see Trudy and unfortunately she's pretty certain she wants to end the placement,' she said. 'She doesn't feel that she can manage Leanne's behaviour any more. Jenny's desperately searching for someone else to take her on long term, but until she finds another carer could she stay with you?'

'Yes, of course,' I said. 'As long as it's only a few days because I was hoping to start that mother and baby placement we talked about.'

'Of course,' replied Becky.

It was sad for everyone when a placement ended abruptly but in this case I felt it was for the best. It seemed like Leanne was the one in control, not Trudy.

'Jenny's over at Trudy's house now getting some of Leanne's stuff, so she'll bring it over to your place later if that's OK?' said Becky.

'That's fine,' I replied.

Leanne had been tricky but I could cope with challenging behaviour if I knew it was only for three or four nights.

Just after lunch Leanne's social worker, Jenny, came round to see me. She couldn't have been any older than her mid-twenties and she was dressed very formally in a suit and blouse.

'Before we have a chat I'll just go and get Leanne's stuff from the car,' she said.

I was expecting nothing more than an overnight bag so I was surprised when, three trips later, there were two suitcases and a pile of boxes in my hallway.

'I'm sorry there's so much stuff,' she said. 'But when I went round to see Trudy she had everything of Leanne's packed up and ready to go.'

'How is she?' I asked.

'She's still very upset,' said Jenny. 'Becky and I tried talking to her but she's made her mind up that she doesn't want to have Leanne back.'

'So what happens now?' I asked.

'I'm going to spend the rest of the day trying to find another carer who is willing to take her on,' she said. 'I know you're a single carer, and I hope I don't offend you by saying this, but ideally I think Leanne is better placed with a couple. Trudy was on her own and she found her too much to cope with.

I think Leanne's behaviour is too much of a challenge for a single carer. Over the years she's gone through a heck of a lot of foster families,' she said.

'How long has Leanne been in the care system?' I asked.

I was curious to know a little bit more about Leanne's background and intrigued how one young person could create so much havoc wherever she went. 'I'm pretty new to the case myself but from what I've read from Leanne's notes, her mum was a teenager when she had Leanne and her little brother,' explained Jenny. 'She had been in the care system all her life and had issues with alcohol and drugs. They were both removed from Mum when Leanne was five and her brother was one and Leanne's been in care ever since.'

'What happened to her brother?' I asked.

'It looks like he went for adoption pretty quickly because of his age but no one was willing to take both of them, so Leanne stayed in the care system. Since then it's been the same pattern,' sighed Jenny. 'No one can cope with her and she's gone from carer to carer. In the six years she's been in care she's had nearly thirty moves.'

'Thirty?' I gasped.

That was a heck of a lot of disruption and upheaval for such a young girl.

'Last year she went through six different carers in as many months,' she added.

I'd fostered several children who had been shunted around the care system but this was unprecedented. My heart went out to this little girl, unwanted and rejected from day one. It was no wonder she was so angry and disruptive and I felt sad that so many carers had given up on her.

The Girl No One Wanted

'She's had a couple of spells in children's homes too but that's never worked out either,' said Jenny. 'She's been with Trudy four months and that's been one of her longest placements. Most people can't seem to cope with her and only last a couple of months.'

I now realised what Trudy had meant when she said that she'd felt sorry for Leanne and I could hazard a guess about where things had gone wrong for her. Like me, Trudy would have heard about this poor eleven-year-old passed from pillar to post for most of her life, rejected by everyone, and she would have given in to her. After all those years in care Leanne knew exactly what buttons to press to provoke a reaction and she had clearly walked all over Trudy. She was a tough placement for anyone, never mind a fairly new, inexperienced carer.

'Why do you think these placements don't last?' I asked.

'She's disruptive,' said Jenny. 'She kicks up a fuss about everything and is very angry. In the past she's lashed out at carers and smashed things up. Understandably, people are not prepared to put up with that sort of aggressive behaviour.'

She was so young yet had caused so much trouble for so many people. It didn't bode well for her future.

'Has she had any therapy or counselling?' I asked.

'I only came to this case four months ago when Trudy was first fostering her, so to be honest I don't know much more than what I've read in her file,' said Jenny. 'I know other social workers have got her some play therapy in the past but I believe she didn't respond well to it so it was stopped after a couple of sessions.'

I felt sad as I got the sense that Leanne was a child who was lost in the system. She'd gone through almost as many social

158

workers as she had homes and there had been zero continuity or stability so far in her young life. She wouldn't have been able to form a proper attachment with anyone because no one had attached to her.

'I've arranged for Leanne to be dropped here after school,' Jenny told me. 'Then I'll come round and talk to her later.'

I suspected Leanne wasn't going to be happy to be coming back to my house so I steeled myself for a meltdown as I saw the taxi pull up outside later that afternoon.

'Why do I have to come back here?' she demanded as she stomped through the front door.

Then she saw the suitcases and boxes in the hallway.

'So she's got rid of me,' she yelled. 'Well I hated her anyway.'

She stormed through to the kitchen and I followed her.

'Leanne, I know you must be feeling really hurt and confused right now and that's OK,' I said, putting a comforting hand on her shoulder.

'No I'm not,' she snapped, shrugging me away from her. 'I told you, I didn't like Trudy. I never want to see her again.'

I poured her a glass of orange squash and got her to sit at the table, and that seemed to calm her down. She stared into space as she drank her juice and ate a Rich Tea biscuit and I could see she was taking in the fact that she wasn't ever going back to Trudy's house.

'So where am I going to go now?' she asked eventually in a quiet voice.

'Jenny's going to come round and talk to you later but for now you're going to be staying with me,' I told her.

'Well I hope she finds me somewhere to go soon 'cause I definitely don't want to stay here long,' she yelled.

I knew her anger was her way of protecting herself. To be honest, knowing what I now did, I couldn't really blame her after a lifetime of moves and insecurity.

'Can I watch TV?' she asked.

'If you want,' I said. 'Or you can help me unpack a few of your things?'

'Nah,' she told me. 'You do it.'

I knew she'd had a tough couple of days so I didn't push her to help me. I didn't think there was any point in unpacking all her stuff if she was only going to be with me for a few days. However, I thought it might be nice to have a few of her things around her and make her feel a little bit more settled.

I lugged all of her stuff upstairs and put it in the spare room. I lifted one of the cases on the bed and unzipped it. Inside there were piles of neatly folded clothes. They were all clean but they were very functional and plain. Looking through them, there was no sense of what Leanne's favourite colour was or what she liked. It was as if someone had gone to the local supermarket and bought a girl's basic wardrobe. Normally I look through a child's wardrobe and I can tell instantly that they love football or Minions, or they like unicorns and their favourite colour is green but there was nothing personal or individual about Leanne's clothes.

Most children in the care system don't tend to have much but nine times out of ten they have some little thing that's special to them such as an old blanket, a grubby teddy or a favourite bracelet. Leanne appeared to have nothing personal. There were no well-loved teddies or dolls, books with worn edges or special blankets. There were no toys, jewellery, colouring books and pens, photographs or drawings. There were basic toiletries in clear plastic wallets, the plainest most functional hair bobbles and a handful of brown kirby grips. Leanne had everything she needed and it was all clean but they were just possessions that had no meaning.

My eyes filled with tears. No matter how she'd behaved, there was nothing here that told me that she had been loved or cared for. I knew Trudy had tried, but Leanne's things showed me that no one had invested in her enough to get to know who she was or what she liked. Not even a teddy for her to cuddle at night.

I had a sense that everyone – from her own mother to social workers and countless foster carers – had given up on Leanne, so she'd given up on them. She'd learnt the most effective ways to push people away was through fear and aggression.

It was no wonder she had problems trusting people. The lesson she had been taught by life was that nobody sticks around and I suspected her behaviour was a way of forcing people to reject her. Her belief was that nobody wanted her so she made sure that was what happened.

Rejection was the only thing that she was sure of in life. It broke my heart wondering if that would ever change.

THREE

Lashing Out

The doorbell rang just as I was putting some of Leanne's clothes into a drawer. Jenny had come round to talk to her.

'She's in the living room,' I told her.

We both walked in to find the telly blaring and Leanne glued to the screen.

'Leanne, Jenny's here to talk to you,' I told her. 'Shall we turn this off?'

She ignored me so I picked up the remote and pressed the 'off' button.

'Hey, I was watching that!' she snapped.

'Hi, Leanne,' smiled Jenny. 'How are you today?'

'I don't wanna talk to her,' she scowled. 'I already know that Trudy doesn't want me any more and I don't care 'cause I hated her anyway.'

I quickly excused myself and disappeared into the kitchen to make a cup of tea. I could tell there was going to be fireworks and I knew this was a matter for Jenny, as her social worker, to discuss with Leanne. As I carried a cup of tea for Jenny back down the hallway, I could hear Leanne ranting and raving about how she didn't want to stay with me. I was about to go back in the living room when the front door opened. It was Louisa back from work. She'd been at her boyfriend's house the previous night so she didn't know about Leanne yet. She raised an eyebrow as she heard the commotion coming from the front room.

'We've got a new placement for a few days,' I told her.

'I can hear that,' she replied.

Just then the living room door flew open and Leanne stormed out.

'I told you I don't wanna stay here,' she yelled, slamming the door behind her.

The sight of Louisa standing in the hallway stopped her in her tracks.

'What are you staring at?' she shouted.

'Nothing,' said Louisa, a surprised look on her face.

Leanne sighed and stomped off upstairs.

'Isn't that the girl from the picnic?' asked Louisa. 'She still seems very angry.'

'Yes, she is,' I told her. 'Let me go and have a word with her social worker and I'll fill you in later.'

After six years of living with me, Louisa was used to all sorts of children turning up unexpectedly. She went into the kitchen while I took in Jenny's cup of tea.

'Well that didn't go well,' she sighed.

'It's understandable after all the moves and upheaval she's had,' I said.

Although Leanne had repeatedly said that she didn't care that she'd left Trudy's, I knew that moving placement again was a huge thing for her. This latest move would have triggered all of her past rejections. She might not have known it but I could tell that somewhere inside her there was a little girl who was desperate to be loved.

'Unfortunately she doesn't seem that happy about staying with you,' said Jenny.

'I won't take it personally,' I smiled. 'To be honest I was expecting that reaction.'

She'd only been at my house for twenty-four hours but Leanne could no doubt already see that I would challenge her rather than bowing down to her demands, and she didn't know what to make of that after Trudy had given in to her for so long.

'Shall I keep sending her to school as normal in the taxi then?' I asked.

'Yes, the school's been informed that she's with you at the minute and they've got your number,' said Jenny.

'Should I prepare myself to be bombarded with calls from them?' I asked.

I knew from experience that children who were in the care system and had had lots of disruption in their lives sometimes struggled to settle in at school and often had behavioural and anger problems.

'Funnily enough, Leanne's never had any issues at school,' said Jenny. 'She hasn't been expelled or excluded and she goes every day without any problem. The one saving grace is that, despite all her moves, Social Services has managed to keep her at the same primary school over the past few years. It's a little bit further away, which is why we organised the taxi to take her to help out Trudy.'

Clearly school was the only consistent thing in Leanne's life. It was her longest and only attachment and I guessed that was probably why she behaved there.

Jenny left shortly afterwards.

'Keep in touch and give me a ring if you need anything,' she said, looking back over her shoulder as she got into her car.

Louisa kindly offered to cook a stir-fry for dinner while I went upstairs to check on Leanne. I knocked on the door and went in to find her lying on the bed.

'How are you doing?' I asked.

'Pissed off 'cause I don't want to stay here,' she whined.

'Look, Leanne, I know that you're hurting, I understand that.'

'No I'm not,' she snapped. 'I hated that bitch. I'm glad she got rid of me.'

'Leanne, you need to mind your language,' I told her. 'You might not like Trudy but I don't want to hear that in my house.'

'I'll say what I want,' she scowled.

I knew there was no point getting into an argument with her but at the same time I wanted to help her process how she was feeling. Sometimes, engaging a child in a task allowed them to talk a bit more freely.

'I tell you what,' I said. 'Please could you help me to put the last few bits of your clothes in the drawers? I started putting them away earlier but I didn't get a chance to finish. I don't want them to get crumpled in the case.'

'No,' she snapped, folding her arms defiantly. 'You do it.'

I felt exasperated.

'They're your clothes, Leanne, and I'd like you to help put them away. I've done most of them so it won't take long.'

'I said no!' she yelled. 'I'm going downstairs to watch TV.'

'Nope, sorry,' I said, blocking her entrance into the hallway. 'The telly doesn't go on until jobs are done, so let's put the clothes away first.'

Leanne kicked out at the chest of drawers in anger but I ignored her and got on with unpacking the last few clothes. She frowned and sighed and huffed and puffed and stood there glaring at me but I didn't say a word. Eventually, after a ten-minute stand-off, she begrudgingly pulled a few clothes out of one of her cases and threw them into a drawer.

'Thank you,' I called as she stomped off downstairs.

Leanne was only going to be with me a few days so I knew I wouldn't have the time to try and tackle her behaviour or get to the root cause of it. But while she was in my house I felt it was important for her to learn that she was the child and I was the adult and therefore I was the one in charge, not her. Even if she was with me for one day she needed to know that her actions had consequences, and no matter how much of a fuss she made I wasn't going to give in to her.

She was clearly determined to push me as far as she could, though. Dinner that night was strained. Again, every little thing was a battle with Leanne. I refused to give in to her requests for something else to eat and drink so she spent the meal glowering into her noodles while Louisa and I chatted. Louisa, bless her, tried to include her whenever she could.

'How long are you staying with us, Leanne?' she asked.

'Hopefully not long,' she frowned, scraping the food around her plate.

'If you could go and live anywhere in the world where would you go?' I joined in.

Sometimes involving kids in fantasy talk was a good way of engaging them.

'Somewhere way nicer than this,' she said. 'A big house with loads of animals.'

'Ah, so you like animals, do you?' I said. 'I'll have to introduce you to our cats Billy and Mog.'

Leanne shrugged and didn't look impressed but at least she had told me one little thing about who she was and what she liked. After dinner I started to clear up.

'As Louisa kindly cooked for us you and I can do the washing up,' I told Leanne. 'I'll wash and you dry.'

'No way,' she said angrily. 'I'm not doing that. It's not my job.'

'It's not anybody's job, Leanne, it's just what we do in this house,' I told her. 'We help each other out where we can.'

'Well I'm not doing it and you can't make me,' Leanne yelled.

'You're absolutely right, I can't make you,' I told her calmly. 'However, the TV won't go on until you've done as I've asked you.'

'That's not fair,' she cried, furious.

'You might not think so but it still needs doing,' I said.

Leanne had to follow the rules like anyone else who came to live with me. It would have been easy to let it slide but I could see that she was so used to being in control and getting her own way by shouting and manipulation. I was determined not to give into her like Trudy and countless other foster carers clearly had.

After a lot of eye rolling, sighing and stamping her feet, she finally picked up a tea towel.

'Thank you, Leanne, that will make everything so much quicker,' I said.

Leanne didn't say a word as she dried the dishes. She slammed each one down on the draining board.

'You seem really cross,' I added. 'You can't possibly be that angry about drying a few dishes. Do you want to talk to me about what's making you cross?'

'No,' she snapped, banging a bowl down on the side.

I wanted to try and reach out to her and let her know I knew how scared she must be feeling.

'I know things haven't been easy for you,' I said gently. 'And I know you must be hurting about having to leave another carer.'

'No I'm not,' she spat. 'I told you, I wanted to go. Trudy was a bitch.'

'It's only natural to be worried about where you're going to be living next,' I said.

'I said I don't f***ing care,' she screamed.

She got the dinner plate that she was drying and hurled it onto the floor where it shattered into pieces. Then she stormed off.

She wasn't the first child I'd looked after who'd broken one of my plates and I knew she probably wouldn't be the last. It was a common way for kids to lash out.

I went and got a dustpan and brush and cleared it up.

'What happened?' asked Louisa, coming into the kitchen. 'I heard a crash.'

'Oh, just a broken plate,' I said. 'Nothing to worry about. Is Leanne OK?'

'Yeah, she seems fine,' she told me. 'She's just watching TV.'

We often talk about kids who have been through trauma as constantly living in fight or flight mode. Leanne was someone who was definitely in permanent fight mode. Smashing the plate had told me that, despite what she'd said, she did care that yet another person had rejected her.

The rest of the evening was a series of battles to get Leanne into the shower and then to bed. When she was finally in her room I went into the living room with Louisa.

'I'm exhausted,' I said, flopping down onto the sofa.

'She's definitely what I'd call a challenge,' Louisa replied.

'At least I've only got to get through another couple of days and then she's leaving,' I sighed.

All I was doing was what I called 'fire fighting' – dealing with the arguments and conflict as they arose rather than addressing the root cause of the problem. I simply didn't have the time needed with Leanne to do anything else.

In my mind I knew exactly why Leanne was behaving like she did – she was in so much emotional pain. In my experience as a foster carer, the louder kids shouted, the angrier they were and the more they were hurting. Of course she cared that someone had rejected her and that she had been moved on again. She behaved the way she did to keep people away. I wasn't getting flustered by her behaviour or giving in to her demands to keep her quiet, and I could tell that had confused her.

The next couple of days were a real test of my patience. Everything with Leanne was an argument, from why she couldn't watch a '15'-rated film to her turning up the radio to loud every time she walked in the room. She was a child who liked to have noise around her at all times. If the telly or the radio weren't on then she was the one creating the noise. It was almost as if she needed it as a distraction to stop her feeling the hurt. I had a constant headache.

Three days passed and I heard nothing from Jenny until a day later when she turned up on the doorstep. It was a Friday and Leanne was at school.

'I was just about to call you,' I told her. 'How are you?'

'Frustrated,' she said. 'I feel like I've been banging my head against a brick wall.'

'That doesn't sound good,' I said, alarm bells ringing.

I made us both a cup of tea and we sat down in the living room.

'Maggie, I've tried and tried but I can't find a foster carer who is willing to take Leanne on,' she said. 'When I tell them even the tiniest bit about her past history, her behaviour and how many moves she's had they don't want to go anywhere near her. She's been through so many carers in the local area and beyond I've literally run out of options.'

'I can totally understand,' I said. 'So what happens now?'

'I had a meeting with my managers this morning and we've decided that the only possible solution is for her to go into a secure unit,' said Jenny.

These sorts of units were high-security children's homes for children whose behaviour was deemed out of control. Children were permanently supervised and weren't allowed to wander around freely. My heart sank.

'Are you really sure that's the right place for a vulnerable eleven-year-old?' I asked, concerned.

'It's the only option we have at this stage and the safest place we can put her,' said Jenny. 'Leanne's been in a children's home before and that didn't work out. She's attacked carers in the past and she can be very volatile,' she added. 'At least in a secure unit there will be very strict rules in place and any aggressive or violent behaviour won't be tolerated.'

Even though I didn't know Leanne well, I knew a secure unit wasn't the right place for her. The children were supervised by a number of staff who all worked different shifts and they weren't allowed to move around as they chose. Unlike a normal house or children's home, bedrooms and doors to the outside would be locked, and they were told which areas they could be in and when.

The units often worked well for disruptive older children who were a danger to themselves or others, but I knew for someone like Leanne, who was hurting so much emotionally, it would be the final nail in the coffin. In a secure unit she would be looked after by a series of people when what she really needed was someone to invest in her, to fulfil that role of a mum or dad and show her that she was worth caring about.

'The issue we have is that the first available place isn't likely to come up for another three months,' said Jenny. 'So I was wondering . . .'

I held my breath, knowing exactly what was coming.

'. . . whether you would be able to foster her until then?'

'Jenny, I'm sorry but I don't think I can,' I told her. 'It's honestly not Leanne's behaviour that puts me off. I've dealt with a lot of children with behavioural problems over the years. But over the past few months Becky and I have been chatting a lot about what sort of direction my fostering is going to take and I've decided to focus on mother and baby placements for a while. In fact, she has one lined up for me that I was waiting to hear about.'

'I understand, Maggie, but please at least think about it and talk to Becky,' she asked. 'I think Leanne would be better off with you than sending her to another children's home for three months before moving her again to a secure unit.'

'OK,' I said, a pang of guilt striking me in the centre of my chest. 'Leave it with me.'

No matter how valid my reasons were, I always felt terrible about turning a child down.

I rang Becky to talk it through with her.

'Jenny's already explained the situation to me,' she said. 'Maggie, I know it wasn't what you'd originally planned but it's only for three months. There will always be mother and baby placements, but I think you'll be really good for Leanne.'

Jenny had clearly been trying to butter her up too.

'What are you worried about?' she asked, sensing my reluctance.

'Well, if I keep her for any length of time then I will want to try and help her and I honestly think that maybe it's all just too little, too late,' I said. 'Leanne's been allowed to go through all these placements causing havoc, and I don't think I can even begin to untangle seven years' behaviour in three months.'

'Maggie, you don't have to,' said Becky. 'Nobody's expecting you to perform miracles with Leanne. You don't have to do any behavioural intervention with her. You'd just be a holding placement until she could go to the secure unit.'

'Becky, you know me,' I sighed. 'I don't work that way. If you're asking me to have this little girl for three months then of course I'm going to start looking at her behaviour and trying to see what needs to change in order to help her in the future.'

'I've only had Leanne for three days and I'm exhausted. This is a girl who other carers have described as volatile, manipulative, aggressive. She's been moved thirty times because they couldn't cope. You saw how frightened Trudy was of her. I'm sure Leanne hasn't even shown us her true colours yet.'

'Anything you can give her before she goes into a secure unit would be a bonus,' said Becky. 'As you're always telling me, it's never too late for a child to change.'

'In this case I'm not so sure,' I said sadly.

Deep down, I knew what Becky was saying was true, though. Even though Leanne was aggressive and argumentative and I was sure I hadn't seen the worst of her behaviour yet, it was my job to give every child the best chance I could.

'OK,' I sighed. 'I'll have her. But only for three months.'

'Thank you,' said Becky gratefully. 'I know Jenny will be relieved. I'll give her a ring now.'

I felt apprehensive at the thought of what the next few weeks might have in store and also what Leanne's reaction would be to the news. The one thing I was sure about was the way that we'd lived these past few days wasn't how I was prepared to live for the next few months. I needed to get to the root of Leanne's behaviour and not just be fighting fires all the time. Instead, I needed to stand firm and attack the blaze head-on and I knew that wasn't going to be easy. What on earth had I done?

FOUR

Pushed to the Limits

I'd never seen anyone as grateful as Jenny was when she came round to speak to Leanne the following day. It was Saturday so she was off school and was busy watching cartoons in the front room.

'Thanks so much again for agreeing to do this, Maggie,' Jenny said.

It was like déjà vu as she walked into the room and asked her to turn the telly off so she could break the news to her.

We had spoken on the phone the previous evening about how Jenny was going to play it and she didn't feel it was appropriate to tell Leanne about the secure unit at this stage.

'Personally, I think she needs to know,' I'd told her. 'We owe it to her to be honest and I think she needs to start taking responsibility for her own behaviour.'

I felt Leanne needed to know that there wasn't a never-ending supply of carers that she could go and live with and keep on behaving like this.

'I don't agree,' Jenny had countered. 'I don't want her to go completely off the rails and react against it or start to get anxious. I'll just tell her we're still looking for a new home for her and she's staying with you for the next few months in the meantime.'

Although I didn't agree with Jenny, she was Leanne's social worker so her decision was final.

Louisa and I laid low in the kitchen while Jenny spoke to Leanne. Leanne was shouting so loudly that we could hear every word she said.

'I don't wanna stay with her until you find me another placement,' she yelled. 'I hate her and I hate that bitch Louisa.'

'What have I ever done to her?' asked Louisa, looking affronted.

'Don't worry, lovey, I don't think she likes me much either,' I smiled.

'Leanne, I'm afraid you don't have much choice,' I heard Jenny telling her.

Suddenly the living room door slammed and I heard Leanne's footsteps running up the stairs. 'I'll just go and have a quick word with Jenny,' I said.

'That went as we expected,' said Jenny, giving me a weak smile. 'At least she knows.'

As I walked Jenny to the front door to see her out it was all quiet upstairs.

'That's a good sign,' Jenny added. 'Give me a ring if there are any problems.'

'I'm sure it will all be fine,' I replied.

I had literally closed the front door and walked back into the kitchen when there was a thud from upstairs.

'What was that?' asked Louisa.

'I'm not sure,' I said. 'But I'd probably better go and check.'

As I walked into the hallway there was several almighty big bangs followed by what sounded like breaking glass. My heart started pounding and I leapt into action.

'Leanne,' I shouted, racing up the stairs. 'Is everything OK up here?'

There was no answer. I ran into her bedroom to be greeted with a scene of utter destruction. Somehow she'd managed to tip the bed over; the wooden bedside table was on its side and had been splintered and the bedside light was smashed to smithereens on the floor. She'd even managed to pull down the curtains from the rail and rip her duvet cover into bits.

'Leanne, what on earth have you done?' I asked.

'I don't want to stay with you,' she screamed, tears running down her face.

Then, much to my horror, she turned round and started bashing her head against the solid bedroom wall.

'Leanne, please stop that,' I begged. 'You're going to hurt yourself.'

I could see she already had. Blood was dripping down her forehead and was smeared on the wall but still she continued to head-butt it.

Bang, bang, bang.

'Leanne, stop!' I cried as she pounded her head against the wall. 'You have to stop this now.'

'No,' she shouted 'No, I won't. You're gonna have to make me.'

Blood was dripping onto the carpet as a sense of panic rose up inside me.

'No!' I shouted. 'Leanne, that's enough!'

But it was as if she was in a trance as she continued to pummel her head against the wall.

There are only certain instances when I would try and restrain a child and a situation where the child is in serious danger of hurting themselves is one of them. I ran over to Leanne and at the same time she spun round and launched herself at me. With arms and legs flailing everywhere, she came at me like an angry whirlwind. I felt a sharp pain as she kicked me in the shin and then grabbed a fistful of my hair and yanked it out of my scalp.

'Leanne, stop!' I yelled, my leg and head stinging. 'I know you're hurting inside but that doesn't mean you can hurt me.'

'I'm not staying with you,' she screamed, digging her nails into my arm until she drew blood.

Thinking fast, I tried the only technique I knew that would safely restrain a child who had lost control. I pulled my arm away from her, turned around and quickly grabbed her duvet that was lying on the bedroom floor. Then, approaching Leanne from behind, I managed to wrap it around her and hold her in a bear hug.

'Get the f***k off me!' she screamed, wriggling and struggling and doing her best to break free while I held on for dear life.

She might only have been small but she was strong. It was impossible for her to lash out with her arms and legs any more because her body was bundled up in the duvet. But she refused to give up, and threw her neck back and tried to head-butt me from behind. Luckily I managed to duck out of the way just in time.

'It's OK, Leanne,' I soothed. 'It's OK.'

'Get off me, you bitch,' she shouted, still struggling. 'Let me go.'

'I can't,' I told her. 'I'm not going to let you hurt yourself, or me for that matter.'

Using all my strength to keep her wrapped in the duvet, I managed to sink down to the floor and pull her with me. I knew that when a child has lost that much control it's a pointless exercise trying to talk to them. You've got to wait for them to tire themselves out and get it out of their system. All I could do was sit there and hold on to her until her anger and rage subsided.

It was only then that I noticed Louisa lurking at the bedroom door, a shocked look on her face as she saw what was going on.

'Are *you* OK?' she mouthed and I nodded.

Leanne was still struggling and fighting against me as I held the duvet around her. There is something about feeling the weight of a blanket or duvet around them that makes children feel secure and I hoped that eventually she would calm down.

As she struggled against me, all I could think was: what on earth have I let myself in for? I knew this was the Leanne that the other foster carers had described. This was the first real rage of hers that I'd witnessed, and frankly it was terrifying. Could I really cope with this for the next few months?

Thankfully, after a while, I felt Leanne's body relax underneath the duvet and she leant back against me. At last she was quiet.

'You're OK,' I soothed. 'It's going to be OK.'

I sat there for a few minutes longer until I was sure that she wasn't going to kick off again.

'Leanne, I'm going to let go of you now,' I told her calmly. 'But if you start lashing out then I will have to restrain you again.'

Very slowly I backed away from her, leaving her wrapped up in the duvet. That way she would be able to unravel herself when she was ready.

I knew from experience that when a young child is coming out of such an intense rage, it can be very disorientating and often they're very tired and confused. As Leanne emerged from the duvet she suddenly became tearful.

'Ow,' she cried. 'My forehead really hurts.'

'I'm going to go downstairs and get some cotton wool and water to bathe it,' I told her. 'Then afterwards I'll take you to hospital.'

'Hospital?' she gasped. 'But I don't wanna go to hospital.'

'Leanne, you've split your head open quite badly and I need to get someone at the hospital to have a look at it,' I said.

As a foster carer I had a duty to get any head injuries checked out.

'Are you OK for me to go downstairs and get some water?' Leanne nodded.

Louisa was waiting in the kitchen looking worried.

'Is she OK now?' she asked.

'I think so,' I said.

'Are you OK?' she added.

'Just about,' I said, giving her a weak smile. 'Her head's a bit of a mess. I think we're going to have to take her to hospital.'

'I can't believe she smashed up her room like that,' Louisa said. 'Are you going to tell her off?'

'There's no point,' I sighed. 'She's very upset and shaken up. She was reacting against the news that Jenny told her.'

How could I tell a child off for hurting themselves or for being upset about being rejected? How could I tell a child off because nobody wanted them?

When I went back upstairs Leanne was still sitting on the floor and she looked very tired and pale. I sat down next to her and she flinched as I carefully dabbed the wound with some cotton wool.

'You've made a bit of a mess of your poor forehead,' I told her gently.

We went downstairs to the kitchen to get her a drink of water before driving to the hospital.

'Are you all right now?' Louisa asked her. 'You were really upset up there.'

'None of your business,' snapped Leanne. 'Why were you watching me?'

While Leanne got her shoes on, I rang my fostering agency to report the incident. As it was Saturday, I got through to the on-call duty social worker and told her what had happened.

'I'm taking her to A&E now,' I said.

'Are you OK, Maggie?' she asked.

'Yes, I think so,' I replied. 'I'm a little bit shaken up but thankfully Leanne has calmed down now. I'll write a full account of the incident tonight and email it to Becky so she has it for Monday.'

I went back into the hallway where Leanne was waiting.

'How are you doing?' I asked her. 'Are you ready to go?'

She shrugged.

'There's nothing to worry about,' I said. 'They'll just want to have a quick look at it and you might need a couple of stitches.'

Leanne didn't say a word in the car and she looked absolutely shattered. I wasn't surprised after the outburst she'd just had.

Thankfully paediatric A&E was fairly quiet so we were seen quickly by the triage nurse.

'Is there any involvement from Social Services?' the nurse asked.

'Yes, I'm Leanne's foster carer,' I told her and I gave her Jenny's name and contact details.

'What happened, darling?' the nurse asked Leanne gently.

'She'll tell you,' she snapped, gesturing to me. 'It's her fault.'

'A social worker came out this morning and gave Leanne some news that she was upset about,' I said.

'No I wasn't!' shouted Leanne.

I ignored her interruption and carried on.

'Let's just say Leanne wasn't terribly happy about finding out she has to stay with me for a while so she decided a bit of head banging was in order.'

The nurse went to have a look at Leanne's head.

'Don't you touch me, you silly cow,' shouted Leanne.

'Well perhaps we'll wait for the doctor to check it later,' the nurse replied brusquely Understandably she looked horrified that a young girl had talked to her so rudely like that.

We went and sat back down in reception to wait and see the doctor.

'Leanne, you can't speak to people like that,' I told her. 'They're trying to help you and they're not going to want to do that if you're being rude to them.'

'Well she shouldn't have touched me,' she snapped.

'Leanne, they're going to have to touch you to check your head,' I said.

Thankfully Leanne managed to hold her tongue by the time we saw the doctor.

'It's not as bad as it looks,' he said. 'We should be able to glue it rather than stitch it.'

'How are you feeling now?' he asked Leanne.

'All right,' she shrugged.

While a nurse sorted out her forehead, the doctor had a chat to me in private.

'As you've told us that this was a self-inflicted injury we also have to make sure that we address the psychological side of things,' he said.

'Of course,' I replied.

'How's her state of mind?' he asked. 'Do you think Leanne is OK going back with you or are you worried that she might hurt herself again?'

'I think she's OK,' I said. 'She got herself so angry and worked up about what her social worker told her this morning but she seems much calmer now.'

I explained that she had only been with me for four days but her behaviour had been quite volatile.

'Would it be possible to get a referral to CAMHS? I think it would be useful for Leanne to have someone to talk to about how she's feeling,' I asked.

CAMHS stood for Children and Adolescent Mental Health Service.

'I can organise that,' said the doctor.

By the time we got back home it was late afternoon and I could tell Leanne was exhausted. Louisa, bless her, had put a casserole in the oven and had tidied up Leanne's room.

'There's still a bit of blood on the carpet that I couldn't get off,' she said.

'Never mind, lovey,' I replied. 'I really appreciate you trying.'

Leanne spent the rest of the afternoon lying on the sofa and watching telly. After the day we'd had I didn't push her to talk, and to be honest I was enjoying the calm after the storm. The following day was the same.

'How's your forehead?' I asked her on Sunday morning as she sat at the table finishing her breakfast.

'I've got a really bad headache,' she sighed, so I gave her some paracetamol. 'What would you like for lunch later?' I asked her as I sorted some washing out for the machine. 'It just struck me today that really I know nothing about you. What do you like to eat?'

'I like roast dinners,' she said meekly.

'OK then,' I said, smiling. 'A roast it is.'

I could see she was still exhausted from her antics the previous day but I wanted to make sure that she was OK mentally as well as physically. I went and sat next to her at the table with my cup of tea.

'You seem a bit calmer today,' I told her. 'You were so angry and upset yesterday. I was really worried about you, you know.'

Leanne shrugged and refused to look at me.

'Has this happened to you before?' I asked gently. 'Have you hurt yourself before?'

'I didn't hurt myself,' she snapped. 'It wasn't me, it was the wall.'

'Well, you had to bang your head against the wall to make it hurt.'

'I don't want to talk about it!' she shouted as she got up from the table and stormed off.

Just as she was about to walk out the door she paused and snapped back at me: 'And I bet you'll be talking to Jenny tomorrow and getting rid of me then won't you?'

'I'm afraid not,' I said. 'You're with me for the next few months, lovey.'

Leanne didn't say a word and marched off to her room.

*

After Leanne had left for school on Monday morning there was a flurry of phone calls. Becky phoned to check I was OK and then Jenny rang.

'How's she doing after this weekend's drama?' she asked.

'Well she's gone off to school quite happily,' I said. 'Her forehead's still sore but thankfully we haven't had any repeat of Saturday's behaviour. In fact she's been extremely quiet all weekend.'

I told her how I'd asked the hospital for a referral to CAMHS.

'I really think she needs it,' I said, sighing.

'I agree,' replied Jenny. 'She's been on the waiting list for the past nine months but I phoned up this morning, and after what happened at the weekend they've given her an emergency appointment in a few days. Is that OK with you?'

'Great,' I said, feeling relieved.

Over the next couple of days Leanne was stroppy, rude and uncooperative. Every single thing was a battle but I was relieved that there weren't any more violent outbursts. I didn't tell her about the appointment with the mental health team until the night before.

'Jenny rang today,' I said casually. 'Tomorrow morning we're going back to the hospital to talk to a doctor about the things that are upsetting you. They want to see if they can help you a bit more so you don't end up hurting yourself again.'

'I told you, it was the wall not me,' she snapped. 'And what about school?'

'I've got permission to take you out for your appointment,' I said.

Leanne was still grumbling about it in the morning.

'But I don't wanna go,' she moaned.

'I'm afraid you don't have a choice,' I said. 'We're going.'

I was relieved that we'd been seen so quickly but I wasn't really sure what they hoped to achieve in an hour's session. Perhaps they were going to offer her some play therapy again, or some talking therapy this time. Whatever they suggested, I knew it couldn't do any harm as Leanne's behaviour was well and truly out of control.

Our appointment was with two male doctors.

'I'm Dr Davies,' one of them told Leanne. 'I'm going to go into another room with Maggie for a little bit so we can have a chat and you can stay and talk to Dr McManus.'

Leanne didn't say a word and I could tell she was nervous.

We went into an adjoining office while Dr Davies took some notes about Leanne and how long she had been with me. He was just asking me what I thought some of her issues were when we heard banging and shouting coming from the room next door. The doctor leapt up and I followed him into the room to see that Leanne had caused complete havoc. She'd ripped posters off the wall, she'd tipped the bin over and pushed over the chair she was sitting on. Now she was kicking the door.

'I want to go now,' she yelled. 'I want to go.'

'Leanne, I'm afraid Dr Davies and I were talking and we haven't finished yet,' I said calmly. 'When the doctors have finished talking to us then we can go.'

'How about we all sit in here together?' said Dr McManus. 'Will you sit down then, Leanne?'

She ignored him and carried on kicking the door.

'OK then,' he said, clearly giving up any hope of Leanne engaging with him and turning to me instead.

'The thing is I'm not sure that there's much we can help with at this stage as I see from the notes Social Services gave us that Leanne's only with you for a short time,' he told me. 'It says here that she's with you for three months until a place in a secure unit becomes available. Is that the case?'

Leanne stopped kicking the door and froze. I knew she had heard every word the doctor said about the secure unit.

'Yes, I believe that's the plan,' I said cautiously.

I held my breath, hardly daring to look at Leanne and what her reaction might be.

The doctor could see from my expression that he'd let slip something that he shouldn't.

'So you're gonna lock me up and put me in a prison?' shouted Leanne, spinning round to face us.

'Leanne, a secure unit isn't a prison,' I told her, desperately trying to calm her down. 'Let's talk about this when we get home.'

The doctor looked uncomfortable and tried to dig himself out of the hole.

'Leanne, I'm sure Social Services are doing their best for you. They just need to find somewhere you can go where you will be safe and looked after.'

Leanne's eyes filled with tears and suddenly she looked so small and vulnerable. I could see the despair and hurt in her face and my heart broke for her.

'I want to go now,' she said, walking towards the door and out into the corridor.

'I'm very sorry about that,' said the doctor to me as I got up to follow her. 'I didn't realise that she didn't know.'

'Don't worry,' I told him. 'She would have to have been told at some point. I'll chat to her when we get home.'

I managed to catch up with Leanne, who was waiting quietly in reception.

As we walked out of the building, she didn't say a word to me.

'Leanne, are you OK?' I asked her but she refused to answer me.

She strode across the car park and slammed the car door shut as she threw herself into the back seat.

'I'm really sorry,' I told her. 'I know you heard some information back there that was a bit of a shock for you.'

But Leanne refused to look at me, never mind speak to me. She sat there in her seat, her arms folded, scowling at the floor. We drove home in silence. All the while I was silently cursing the doctor for dropping this bombshell. Why didn't he think before he said it? I knew Jenny wasn't going to be happy about Leanne finding out. This is why I insisted that it was always best to be honest with children.

When we got home, the house was quiet as Louisa was at work.

Leanne stomped through the front door and into the kitchen. I followed her.

'Sit down, Leanne,' I said, as she paced up and down. 'I know you're upset but I'll make us a drink and we'll talk about this and I can explain to you what a secure unit is.'

'I know what it is,' she said. 'It's a prison, isn't it? I'm so bad you're all going to lock me up.'

'Oh, Leanne, no one's going to lock you up,' I told her.

I turned round to flick the kettle on as I was desperate for a cup of tea. When I turned back, Leanne was standing in front of me, her blue eyes filled with tears and an angry look on her face. It was then that I noticed she was holding something in her right hand.

A large silver carving knife glistening in the light.

She must have picked it up from the draining board when I had my back to her.

My heart started thumping as I saw the look of utter anger and contempt on her face as she walked towards me. Inside I was panicking but I knew I had to stay calm.

'Leanne, I know you're upset but put the knife down,' I said.

'Did you know?' she shouted, waving the knife around. 'Did you know they were going to lock me up forever?'

'Leanne, no one's going to lock you up forever,' I told her. 'A secure unit is a special kind of children's home.'

'I said did you know?' she hissed, edging further towards me.

My heart was racing. I had to be honest with her – if she knew I was lying God only knew what she might do.

'Yes, I did know but I didn't know a great deal about it,' I told her. 'I knew that was what Jenny was thinking as she wanted to keep you safe.'

'But I don't want to be locked up forever,' she screamed. 'I don't want to be locked up.'

I pressed my back against the kitchen unit as she edged closer and closer towards me, the carving knife waving around in her hands.

FIVE

Lost Little Girl

As Leanne came towards me, the blade of the knife glinting in the light, I didn't dare move an inch. My heart was pounding and I was too afraid to even blink, for fear of what Leanne might do. She was shaking like a leaf and I could tell that she had completely lost all control. The only saving grace was that Louisa was safely out of the way at work.

'Leanne, please put the knife down so we can talk,' I said, desperately trying to sound calm even though inside I was terrified.

'I told you, I don't want to be locked up,' she screamed.

Trying not to make any sudden movements that could send Leanne into a panic, I ran through different scenarios in my head. I didn't want to tackle her and try to get the knife off her as she might lash out, and one or both of us could get hurt. Yes, she was slight and smaller than me, but she was angry and upset and she had a carving knife in her hand. How could I defend myself?

If she did come towards me then I could duck or roll on the floor and try to crawl away but I didn't want to let it get to that.

I knew in reality all I could do was remain calm and in control. I hoped that in talking to her, she would put the knife down.

'Leanne, I can see why you're upset,' I told her. 'But I can't talk to you while you're waving that knife around. Put the knife down, Leanne.'

I was deliberately using calm and repetitive language, as that was what I'd been taught in my training in order to defuse a situation and help bring the child back to reality.

She doesn't really want to hurt me, I tried to convince myself.

She was frightened and distressed and had picked up the closest thing to hand.

'It's all your fault,' she said, still waving the knife at me. 'I bet it was your idea to lock me up.'

I knew she was angry because at that moment I represented social workers, foster carers, anyone and everyone who had ever rejected her. This was her tipping point, all of her anger about being in care was coming out. She believed that we were going to lock her up and throw away the key and understandably that had sent her over the edge.

'Leanne, you must listen to me,' I told her. 'Put the knife down and give me a chance to talk to you about this and explain what a secure unit really is.'

But she wasn't listening. It was like she was in some sort of trance as she paced up and down in front of me. Then suddenly she stopped and the tears came.

'I don't want to be locked up,' she sobbed. 'Please don't lock me up.'

She crumpled to the floor on her knees and dropped the knife. I quickly grabbed it and shoved it out of the way in a high cupboard then ran back to comfort her.

She sank into me as I put my arms around her.

'I'm scared, Maggie,' she sobbed, her body shaking. 'Please don't lock me up.'

'It's OK, Leanne,' I soothed, stroking her hair. 'It's OK.'

She looked like a lost little girl and my heart went out to her as I could see she was genuinely frightened. I held her until her tears turned to whimpers and then finally to silence.

'Leanne, if you don't want to go to a secure unit what do you want?' I asked her gently.

She shrugged.

'You need to tell us, lovey,' I said. 'You need to tell me and you need to tell Jenny.'

She sunk her head down to her chest and refused to look at me.

'What do you want?' I asked her again.

'I want a mum and a dad that love me,' she said. 'I want a house and some roller boots.'

Then she burst into tears again. It was the first time she'd let her barriers down and shown me her vulnerable side. It was heartbreaking because the bottom line was she wanted to belong and have people who loved her. She didn't want to be the girl no one wanted.

I cuddled her until the tears subsided and she was quiet again.

'In a little while I'm going to ring Jenny, because I think it's very important that she comes round and explains to you about secure units,' I said. 'In the meantime I'm going to run you a bath.'

We were both very shaken up by what had happened and I found baths were a good way to calm kids down and relax them.

With Leanne in the bath it also gave me time to try and get my head together and process what had just happened. It was only when she was out of my sight that I allowed myself to relax and I realised that I was shaking. I sat down in the kitchen, closed my eyes and took a few deep breaths.

I'm OK, I told myself, we're both OK.

Once the moment had passed I leapt straight into organisational mode. The first thing I did was remove the knife block from the work surface and lock it away in a cupboard. Then I rang Jenny.

She seemed more bothered by the fact the doctor had let slip about the secure unit than Leanne threatening me with a knife.

'What on earth was he thinking?' she huffed.

'This is the reason why I think it's important to tell kids the truth from the beginning, because you can't control what other people are going to say and do,' I said. 'It's not worth the risk.'

I couldn't openly criticise a social worker to her face but I was annoyed that her decision had put me in real danger.

'I'll come round now,' sighed Jenny, clearly exasperated.

Leanne was very quiet by the time she got out of the bath. She didn't even put up much resistance when Jenny arrived, which wasn't like her. I left them to it and when I came back in Leanne was crying again.

'But I don't want to go,' she sobbed.

'I know you don't like it, Leanne, but we honestly don't know what else to do,' Jenny told her. 'I'm afraid you've burnt all your bridges and we don't have a family to take you. We have a responsibility to keep you safe and this is the only way I can see that happening.'

While I got Leanne a drink Jenny and I had a chat in the kitchen.

'You've got to remember that she's only eleven,' I told her. 'I know her behaviour is a pain in the bum but at the end of the day she's still a child.'

'I think it's a bit more than being a pain in the bum, Maggie,' she said. 'Look at what happened this morning.'

'If you're telling her there's no other option than to send her to a secure unit then what reason has she got now to try and change?' I asked. 'How about negotiating with her that if she goes to the secure unit for a set period of time and she gets her behaviour under control then you'll happily explore the possibility of a family for her in the future?'

I felt sad that at the age of eleven her hopes of ever having a family of her own were being taken away from her. My firm belief is that, wherever possible, every child no matter what their age has the right to a family, and you should never give up hope.

'Maggie, her behaviour is completely out of control,' said Jenny. 'She can't be pulling knives on people and then expect us to find her the perfect family, can she?'

'But you have to look at what had just happened,' I told her. 'She'd just been given some information by a complete stranger that had completely shocked her. She didn't know what a secure unit was. As far as she was concerned, she was going to be sent away and locked up in some sort of a prison. Yes, her behaviour isn't great but in my eyes she's been let down by the system.'

'Today has only made me more convinced that a secure unit is the best place for her,' said Jenny, sounding affronted that I was daring to challenge the system that she was part of.

*

Even after Jenny left, my head was buzzing. No matter what had happened today, I was still convinced a secure unit wasn't the right place for Leanne to spend the rest of her childhood. At eleven she would be one of the youngest there and her role models would be older, potentially more disruptive and violent kids.

The rest of the day passed in a blur. Both Leanne and I were exhausted after the intense drama of the morning. Louisa was staying at her boyfriend's and I didn't want to call and worry her with what had happened. I'd phoned my agency and Becky was coming round in the morning to have a chat and do another risk assessment.

That night I struggled to sleep. I kept going over and over what had happened in my head. Was it my fault? Was there something I could have done differently? I couldn't help but imagine how easily things could have ended very badly. It didn't bear thinking about.

When Leanne had gone off to school, Becky arrived.

'I'm sorry to hear about what happened yesterday, Maggie,' she said. 'How are you?'

'I'm OK,' I said. 'It was a bit of a shock, to say the least, but thankfully it all ended fine.'

I knew Becky needed to deal with the practical side of things. There was the possibility she could do a risk assessment and say it was too dangerous for Leanne to stay. I had to bow to her judgement; sometimes as a foster carer you can get so caught up in wanting to help a child whereas she was looking at the harsh reality.

'The knives are all safely locked away in a cupboard now,' I said. 'So it can't happen again.'

'Yes, Maggie, but you and I both know anything can be a weapon,' she replied. 'You can't lock everything away. Next time it could be a vase or a glass or a brick from the garden. Perhaps I got this wrong and you shouldn't be doing this twelve weeks with Leanne,' she said. 'Maybe her behaviour is too out of hand and it's not fair to put either of you in danger.'

'Honestly, Becky, it's fine,' I told her. 'There's no denying that the incident yesterday was frightening. But we got through it and after it had happened it was more about comforting and calming her. I don't feel anxious about having her in the house or worried about my or Louisa's safety.

'You and I both know that children's actions are mostly born out of fear, and Leanne was absolutely terrified,' I added. 'She'd just been told out of the blue that she was going to a secure unit and it had completely thrown her. There was no intent or malice about her actions. She hadn't pre-planned to grab a knife and thought about ways to stab me. It was a reaction, an in-the-moment thing.

'She's a scared little girl and I desperately want to try and help her,' I said.

It was only as I said the words out loud that I realised how invested in Leanne I'd become. In the first instance, offering her a home had never been what I'd wanted but, despite my best intentions, I'd become emotionally attached to this troubled little girl and I wanted the best for her. Above all, I so desperately wanted to help her.

'As long as you're sure,' said Becky.

'I am,' I said. 'I'm not expecting miracles but I'm going to give it a damn good go.'

I was sufficiently experienced to know that twelve weeks wasn't long enough to fix a lifetime's worth of damage but I hoped I could make some tiny difference to Leanne. All I could do was hold a mirror up to her and say 'look what you're doing'. This would probably be the first time someone had challenged Leanne's behaviour and I knew she wasn't going to take kindly to it. But I was determined to try.

Sure enough, as the days passed, she threw everything she had at me. Every single thing was a battle, from putting on her shoes in the morning to brushing her teeth at night. I was determined to nip it in the bud and I knew in order to do that I had to stand firm.

The next few weeks consisted of lengthy stand-offs that sometimes lasted more than an hour. Like asking her to make her bed in the morning.

'I don't want to,' scoffed Leanne. 'You can't make me.'

'Well, there isn't a choice and if you don't want to do that then we're just going to stand here and wait until you do,' I told her.

'I'm not doing it,' she replied.

'As I said before, I'm going to stand here until you do,' I repeated.

There was a pile of books on the landing to remind me to take them back to the library. So I grabbed one of them off the top and started reading it aloud. Leanne looked confused.

'What are you doing?' she shouted. 'What are you reading that for?'

'Well if we're both going to stand here for ages we might as well have something to occupy us,' I said, continuing with the story.

It was a good hour before Leanne finally gave in and made her bed.

'I'm gonna be late for school now,' she said as I finally rang for her taxi to come and pick her up.

'I'm afraid that was your choice, so you can explain it to your teacher,' I replied.

At night when I put her to bed she refused to stay in her bedroom. Louisa and I were sitting downstairs one evening when we heard her banging around on the landing.

'You need to be in bed,' I told her.

'No, I'm not tired,' she scoffed. 'If you put me back I'll just come out again.'

So instead I put a stool on the landing outside her bedroom door.

'What's that for?' she asked.

'I'm going to sit here and make sure that you stay in your bedroom,' I said. 'I've got some knitting to keep me busy. So, please, get yourself back to bed.'

She sighed and stropped off into her bedroom. Five minutes later she wandered out onto the landing.

'What do you need, Leanne?'

'Oh, nothing, I was just . . .'

'Just what?'

'I just needed the toilet.'

'Well, go and then get back into bed,' I said.

Over the next two hours I'm not exaggerating when I say Leanne probably went to the toilet at least sixteen times. I knew she was testing me but I refused to leave my seat.

'This is getting ridiculous, Leanne,' I told her. 'If you really need to wee this many times then you're obviously drinking too much.'

'Are you going downstairs yet?' she snapped.

'I'm going nowhere,' I replied. 'As I told you before, I'm going to sit outside your room until you stay in it and go to sleep.'

I could tell that she couldn't quite believe that I was doing this and again she was confused that I hadn't given in to her. I sat outside her room until 1 a.m. when she finally fell asleep. I did the same thing the following night, although thankfully she fell asleep an hour earlier.

Although she didn't admit to it, part of me thought Leanne might be seeking a little bit of comfort too. She was feeling vulnerable and insecure and got comfort from knowing that I was there sitting outside her bedroom until she went to sleep.

There were still daily tantrums and rages to deal with too. One Saturday morning she was laying into Louisa because she said she was staring at her. She smashed a cup and was ranting and raving.

'Stop this, please, Leanne,' I told her but she carried on.

I picked up a cookery book that was close to hand and slammed it down hard on the breakfast bar. The noise made us all jump and Louisa looked at me like I was mad.

'What did you do that for?' snapped Leanne.

It was a shock tactic. If a child is going off on one and they're not listening to you then a loud noise stops them from what they're doing. It takes them out of the moment and resets their brain. Quite often, if I want a younger child's attention and they're not listening to me then I'll clap my hands loudly like a seal. It's about grabbing someone's attention and moving them out of the moment they're in.

'OK, Leanne we're supposed to be going to the cinema later, aren't we?' I said and she nodded.

'However, you have a choice, and if you carry on behaving like this and being nasty to Louisa then I'm not going to take you. Do you want to go to the cinema?'

'Yes,' she muttered.

'Well think about how you're behaving, then.'

As something was about to unfold, it was to do with pointing out to Leanne that actually she did have a choice. She could choose to have a massive temper tantrum or she could choose to let it go and move on. It was about getting her to channel her volatile behaviour and use words instead. It was about taking the bull by the horns and telling her really clearly what the consequences of her behaviour were going to be.

She'd never been forced to take responsibility for her actions before now so this was a slap in the face.

'Why are you so mean to me, Maggie?' she asked before storming out of the kitchen.

I really wanted to help her but trying to change children's behaviour was such hard work. Leanne needed to know that I was in control and not her. And that's the end of the matter.

'I know it has to be done but I feel like such a horrible person,' I said to Louisa. 'It's soul destroying, not to mention exhausting.'

Later on that day Leanne blew a gasket because I asked her to put her coat on.

'OK, this can go one of two ways,' I told her. 'You can have a meltdown, throw things around the room or smash stuff. I can grab that blanket over there, wrap it round you and you can cry. It can all be resolved like that. Or you can just say OK, I'll put my coat on, and we can go out now.'

The Girl No One Wanted

Leanne looked at me, stunned, not sure what to say. A few minutes later, she put on her coat without a word and we went off to the cinema.

That night I popped my head around her bedroom door to say goodnight. Leanne was lying in bed with a very serious look on her face.

'You look very deep in thought,' I said. 'Are you OK?'

'Maggie, why haven't you got rid of me like all the others?' she asked.

I was shocked; it had come completely out of the blue. I went and sat on her bed.

'Because I like you,' I said. 'And because it's my job to look after you. Why would I get rid of you?'

'Because I get so mad all the time and do silly things,' she said.

'We all get mad sometimes,' I said. 'It's just learning about how to control it and using your words instead of getting angry and doing silly things. Are you angry now?' I asked her.

She shook her head.

'No,' she said. 'I'm scared.'

'What are you scared of, sweetie?' I asked.

'I'm scared of going to that prison place,' she said. 'I don't want to be locked up.'

My heart felt heavy for her. No matter how many times Jenny or I had reassured her, the thought of the secure unit was preying on her mind every day.

'I know it sounds scary,' I said. 'But a secure unit isn't a prison, lovey. It's a place to keep you safe and there will be lots of other children there.'

'I don't want to go,' she said.

'It's still a long way off,' I told her as reassuringly as I could, although in my head I knew the time would be here soon enough.

Those first few weeks with Leanne felt like I was wading through mud, but after a couple of months I finally felt like we'd turned a corner. It had been weeks since I'd had to sit outside her bedroom at night and she went to sleep now without any problems. In the morning she happily got herself ready for school and brushed her teeth and hair without any tantrums or meltdowns. All little things but it made life so much easier and happier for all of us. When Becky called one morning, I couldn't wait to update her.

'Have you been reading my recordings?' I told her. 'The dramas are still happening but they're much more short-lived and she's not flying off the handle as much. I mean, I'm not a miracle worker but it's good to celebrate the little victories, isn't it?'

'Maggie, that's great but I've got something to tell you,' she said.

I could tell by the tone of her voice that I wasn't going to like it.

'What?' I asked. 'What is it?'

'I'm sorry to do this to you,' she said. 'But I'm afraid it's not good news. Leanne has made an allegation of assault against you,' she told me. 'She claims that you pushed her down the stairs.'

SIX

Positive Steps

'What?' I gasped, reeling in total and utter shock at Leanne's allegation. 'When is this incident supposed to have happened?'

'Sometime last week,' she said. 'She made the accusation to a teacher at school this morning and the teacher phoned Social Services.'

I couldn't believe what I was hearing.

'That's ridiculous, Becky,' I said. 'You know as well as I do that she's lying. I would never do that.'

'I know that, Maggie – but as you know it's got to be properly investigated through the right channels,' she said. 'Jenny is about to go up to the school and speak to her. Let's keep in touch and I'll call you when I know more.'

Assault was a serious allegation, so Jenny would have to decide whether it was safe for Leanne to come back to the house or not.

I put the phone down feeling hurt and upset as I'd never had an accusation made against me before. I had thought I was making progress with Leanne and was finally getting through to her. Clearly I had it all wrong.

I made sure my mobile was on and went round to have a coffee with my friend Vicky. She was as shocked as I was when she heard what had happened.

'I really felt like we'd turned a corner these past few weeks,' I told her. 'She'd started to let her barriers down and open up to me.'

'That's probably why she's done it,' said Vicky. 'Maybe she feels out of control and this is her way of showing that she still has power.'

I suspected that she was probably right. Leanne had let her guard down and shown her vulnerable side and now she was punishing or testing me.

'Regardless of what it's about it's never a nice experience to be investigated by your superiors,' I sighed. 'Plus it will remain on my permanent record.'

'They will soon be able to tell that she's made it up,' said Vicky.

'I hope so,' I said. 'But Jenny doesn't really know me and often with these cases social workers tend to think there's no smoke without fire.'

'Yes, but Becky does and she'll fight your corner,' reassured Vicky. 'You've got nothing to hide.'

I knew she was right but I was starting to feel weary at this constant drama.

Jenny rang me early that afternoon when I was back at home.

'This is absolute nonsense, you must realise that,' I told her.

'Maggie, you know there's a procedure and I'm obliged to follow it.'

'I know,' I sighed. 'It's just very frustrating.'

Jenny explained that she'd been up to Leanne's school to talk to her.

'She claimed the incident happened last Friday between 4 and 5 p.m. She said she'd got home after school and you were arguing because she wouldn't put her school bag away and you pushed her down the stairs and she fell and hurt her knee.'

I wracked my brains desperately trying to think what we were doing the previous Friday at that time.

'Let me grab my diary,' I said.

I quickly flicked through the pages, frantically trying to jog my memory until I found the right date.

Bingo!

'It couldn't have happened because we were at the doctor's last Friday,' I said. 'We weren't even at home. I got Leanne an appointment as she'd had a rash on her arms for a while. It turned out to be eczema and we were there ages. Her appointment was at 3.45 p.m. but they were running late. Just check with the GP's surgery.'

'OK,' she said. 'Leave it with me and I'll have to talk to Leanne again.'

It was a couple more hours until Jenny phoned back.

'Well?' I asked. 'What did Leanne say?'

'The doctor's surgery confirmed your appointment and when I challenged Leanne about it she admitted that she'd made it all up.'

'What a waste of everyone's time,' I couldn't help but snap. 'Did she say why she'd lied?'

'She didn't,' said Jenny. 'But she was very tearful and upset. I offered to pick her up from school today and bring her back to you instead of the taxi but she said she was fine to come back on her own. I'm really sorry, Maggie, but as you'll appreciate we have to take things like this seriously.'

'I understand,' I said.

I wasn't cross with Leanne, just frustrated that she was still intent on causing all these dramas. When she got back from school she was very sheepish.

'Have you had a good day?' I asked her.

'Not really,' she said meekly.

'Leanne, why did you make those things up?' I asked. 'You know I'd never hurt you.'

'You were annoying me,' she snapped. 'You're always telling me what to do.'

'I can understand why I've irritated you but you have to realise that you can't go round making things up. Especially not serious things like that that will stay on my permanent record forever. Have you done that before?'

I could tell by the way her cheeks went red that she had.

'So now you're finally going to get rid of me, are you?' she snapped.

'No such luck,' I said. 'I'm afraid you're with me for a little while longer. You're not getting rid of me that easy.'

Leanne gave me a weak smile.

'You can always complain if you're upset about something or have a problem' I said. 'It's really important that you feel people are listening to you but please make sure you tell the truth.'

The more I thought about it, the more I suspected Vicky had been right. Perhaps Leanne was feeling vulnerable because she didn't feel in control of things, so by making something up like that she felt she held the power.

Whatever the reasons, I knew we had to put this behind us and move forward. I couldn't afford to hold a grudge. Leanne had another four weeks with me and there was still a lot I wanted to do before she went off to the secure unit.

The Girl No One Wanted

*

At the same time as working on her behaviour, I also knew how important it was to build up her sense of self. I wanted to help her feel like she was an individual worth caring about.

One weekend I took her shopping for some clothes. I wasn't going to spend hundreds of pounds on a whole new wardrobe but I wanted her to choose a couple of things that she liked rather than just because they fitted her.

Most young girls leapt at the chance to go shopping but Leanne wandered around Marks and Spencer looking completely bewildered and overwhelmed.

'What's wrong?' I asked.

'I don't know what to pick,' she replied, looking quite upset about it.

'What sort of things do you like?' I said, trying to encourage her.

'I don't know,' she shrugged. 'No one's asked me to choose clothes before or taken me shopping. They've just given me stuff to wear.'

'What's your favourite colour?' I asked.

Even that seemed like a difficult question for her to answer.

'Purple I think,' she said.

'Well that's a start,' I smiled. 'Let's see if there are any nice purple clothes.'

After much agonising, we ended up coming away with a purple skirt and a unicorn top. I hadn't spent more than £20 but I could see they meant the world to her as she wanted to wear them straight away. I also got her to choose a new duvet cover, which she loved.

That night at bedtime she was very quiet.

'Are you OK?' I asked her. 'Did you enjoy shopping today?'
She nodded.

'I really like the things I got,' she said. 'I just feel sad that I won't be able to take them to the lock-up place.'

'Of course you'll be able to take your things with you,' I said. 'They're yours, you chose them and you get to keep them forever.'

'Really?' she asked, her face brightening.

'Really,' I smiled.

'Epic,' she grinned. 'Thanks, Maggie.'

I also ordered her a pack of pencils and a matching case with her name on.

The false accusations aside, her behaviour had also got much better. Don't get me wrong, there were still dramas and tantrums. One day she punched the wall and I'd lost count of how much of my crockery she'd smashed up in a temper. However, these episodes were a lot less frequent and when they did happen they were over much quicker. There was still the odd battle, but not about every single thing.

It was the little things that showed me she was progressing.

'I've just got to go round to Vicky's house and drop this baby bouncer off,' I told her one evening after dinner.

Vicky's had broken and she'd got a baby coming on a respite placement for a few weeks. I steeled myself for the moaning about do I have to come, the battle for Leanne to get her shoes on and then to get her in and out of the car. I'd warned Vicky I might be a while.

'OK,' said Leanne, happily putting her trainers on. I was flabbergasted. It was only a simple thing but she'd done it without any fuss or arguments.

She stopped kicking off about trips to the supermarket because she accepted that we needed to do things like shopping because we had to eat. Yes, it might be boring, but she understood it was necessary and that then we could move onto something else more interesting.

One morning at breakfast I had to go into the front room to take a call from my fostering agency. I walked back in to find a piece of toast on my plate.

'Thanks, Louisa,' I said.

'Oh, it wasn't me,' she said. 'Leanne made it for you.'

'Really?' I said, sounding more surprised than I intended to. 'That's really kind, thank you.'

Leanne flashed me a proud smile.

We also discovered that Leanne loved decorating cakes. She enjoyed icing them and I showed her how to use a piping bag and all the nozzles to make different patterns.

Jenny popped round one afternoon when Leanne was in the middle of icing a chocolate cake.

'Look at what Leanne's done,' I said, leading her through to the kitchen. 'She's put her name on it.'

'That's really lovely,' said Jenny. 'I love baking too. Every year I make my mum and my sister a birthday cake and I'm always making them for my friends.'

'Do you use a piping bag?' asked Leanne cautiously.

'I do,' said Jenny. 'And sometimes I even use glitter icing.'

'You can get glitter icing?' gasped Leanne, her eyes widening.

'Yep,' said Jenny. 'And sometimes I pipe little flowers around the edges. Do you want me to show you how I do it?'

Leanne nodded. I handed Jenny an apron and she got stuck in.

As I watched them, I realised that was the first time that Jenny had had a personal conversation with Leanne. It was nice to see them talking about something that didn't involve Social Services or secure units. Somehow amongst all the official stuff they had forged a little bond over their common interest.

'Next time I come I'll bring you a copy of the baking magazine I subscribe to,' Jenny told Leanne. 'It teaches you all sorts of tricks.'

'Thanks,' she smiled.

The fact that they could relate to each other about cake-making meant Jenny started to see her as a child rather than just a client, and a problem one at that. In my experience that makes such a difference when you've got social workers working with kids.

When Leanne had finished icing her cake she went upstairs to her room, giving Jenny and me the chance to have a quick chat.

'She's making great progress,' I told her.

'I can see she's really trying,' agreed Jenny.

Now was the time to ask the question that had been preying on my mind for the past couple of weeks.

'As she's come on so much do you think it's worth reconsidering the idea of a secure unit?' I asked. 'What about having another look around to see if there are any carers who will take her?'

'Maggie, I'm being realistic here,' sighed Jenny. 'Yes, Leanne has made great progress with you but she's still a very challenging and difficult child and she always will be. Nothing is going to change what's on her file from her past placements, all the moves she'd had and what happened earlier on when she was first with you.

'Most foster carers are going to take one look at that and run a mile,' she added. 'It's the same problem that I had before. It's too late I'm afraid, Maggie. My managers and I decided a unit was the best way to proceed and there's nothing I can see that will change that.'

It made me feel so sad that a child's future had been written off at age eleven but I knew I was fighting a losing battle. There was literally nothing I could do except get through my last few weeks with Leanne.

One afternoon Becky gave me a call.

'Maggie, we've got a course going on next week and I wondered if you could come in and give a talk?' she asked.

'No problem,' I said. 'Leanne will be at school and, as you know, I quite enjoy it.'

When people applied to be foster carers, one of the things they had to do was to go on a 'skills to foster' training course. As part of that I went in and talked to them about the realities of fostering and what it was like and they could ask me any questions.

We started off the session by sitting around the table and introducing ourselves. I went first.

'I'm Maggie,' I said. 'I've been a single foster carer for more years than I can remember. I've got a young woman who has remained with me since she left the care system and a very challenging eleven-year-old who's with me for a few more weeks until a place comes up in a secure unit.'

We went round the table and everyone introduced themselves. There were four couples all in their thirties and one slightly older pair.

'I'm Julie,' said the lady. 'For the past fifteen years I've worked with young offenders but I've recently left my job as I've made the decision that I want to foster full-time. Steve's in the probation service.'

We also talked about the kinds of children they might be willing to foster. As tends to be the case, the majority of the couples wanted babies and toddlers except Julie and Steve.

'We don't have any illusions of cute little babies or toddlers,' smiled Julie.

'We've got two grown-up lads and I'm not sure we could cope with nappies and bottles now,' laughed Steve.

'I think we're happy to take on older kids, teenagers maybe, with problems. I think our day jobs have prepared us for that. Although I must admit after two boys, I'd love to foster a girl at some point,' said Julie.

It was refreshing to hear that they had such a realistic perspective about fostering and I instantly warmed to them.

After the session Julie came over to see me.

'It was really lovely to meet you, Maggie,' she said. 'Thanks very much. It was really useful to actually speak to someone who fosters.'

'That's not a problem,' I smiled.

Afterwards I had a debrief with Becky to see if I'd picked up any issues with the people that worried me.

'What did you think of Julie and Steve?' she asked me.

'I really liked them,' I said. 'They seemed very warm and her humour was very similar to mine.'

'I think they'll be a real asset to the agency,' she said. 'As you know we're crying out for carers like them who have professional knowledge of managing difficult young people. They can definitely transfer those skills to fostering and it's great they're willing to consider giving older kids a home too.'

I completely agreed.

'How far are they away from approval?' I asked.

'They're going to panel in just under two weeks,' she said. 'They shouldn't really be doing the course this late but they missed the last one because of work commitments.'

I didn't think any more of it. But that night as I lay in bed, I couldn't stop thinking about Julie and Steve and what they had said. They were willing to consider older children, they were used to working with troubled young people with problems, and Julie was keen to foster a girl. And just like that, a little light bulb went off in my head.

SEVEN

Never Too Late

In the days after I'd met Julie and Steve, I couldn't get the thought that they would make the perfect foster carers for Leanne out of my head. But would they even consider taking her on with her past history? Given their inexperience, would Jenny even be willing to explore the idea?

As a foster carer I don't have the power to decide what happens to a child. I can make suggestions but ultimately the local authority and the child's social worker have parental responsibility so they make the decisions. I knew, after doing this job for many years, all I could do was talk to Becky and then hopefully she would agree to sow the seeds of my idea to Jenny.

The following week I had a supervision session booked in with Becky.

'So Leanne's only got a few more weeks with you before her place at the secure unit comes up,' she said. 'How are you feeling about things?'

'If I'm being honest I feel really upset about it,' I told her. 'Leanne has improved enormously from how she was when she first came to me and I'm sad for her that she doesn't have any other option than to go into a unit.'

'I know that Social Services has tried but there aren't any carers who will take Leanne, given her past history,' she said.

'What about that couple that came to the training session the other day?' I suggested casually. 'Julie and Steve, I think it was. I definitely think they would be worth looking at. Their experience sounds perfect.'

'Maggie, are you meddling again?' she smiled. 'The last time I looked I don't think your job description involved arranging placements.'

'It was just a suggestion,' I said innocently. 'A suggestion I was hoping you might be able to make to Jenny. You could make it seem like it's coming from you.'

'OK, I'll mention it to her,' said Becky. 'Although I'm not promising anything. The last time we discussed this she still seemed very intent that the unit was the way forward.'

'Thank you,' I said. 'I appreciate you trying.'

I'd put so much time and energy into trying to help Leanne I didn't want her to go into a unit and destroy all the good work that she'd done. I felt that she deserved to have a chance at life with a family.

Another couple of weeks passed and I didn't hear anything back from Becky. I was under no illusion that this might actually be taken seriously and I assumed Jenny had dismissed the idea.

Jenny phoned as usual one afternoon.

'I had an interesting chat with Becky the other day,' she said. 'She was telling me that there's a couple who are about to be approved to foster who are used to dealing with difficult children. One of them works in the probation service, apparently, and the other in remand.'

'Oh yes,' I said innocently. 'I think she means Julie and Steve. I met them on a training course a few weeks ago. I really liked them. So what were you thinking?' I asked. 'Do you think it's worth looking at them as prospective foster carers for Leanne?' I couldn't dance around the subject any longer.

'That was what Becky was suggesting but I'm in two minds,' said Jenny. 'How do we know they'll be able to manage her behaviour? Trudy was inexperienced and look how that turned out.'

'With the kind of jobs they do they'll have had all the training,' I replied. 'They must be used to young people pushing the boundaries.'

In my mind, we couldn't have handpicked any better carers.

'Yes, but there's a big difference between having that at work and then having someone in your own home 24/7 causing chaos.'

'But look how far Leanne has come,' I told her. 'Her behaviour isn't perfect but it's so much better than when she first came to me.'

'It is,' said Jenny.

Then she paused.

'Maggie, she's obviously doing so well with you. Are you sure you won't reconsider and keep her on long term? This is the first placement she's had where she's made any real progress.'

'Jenny, you know my feelings about this,' I said. 'Mother and baby placements are what I want to be focusing on at the moment and if I had Leanne I wouldn't be able to do that. Besides, Leanne has told me what she wants. She wants a family with a mum and a dad and I'd love for her to be able to have that.'

'I understand,' said Jenny. 'I just wanted to ask and see if anything had changed.'

I had the same old feelings of guilt but it was important that I had choices too about where my life was going. I was initially just a holding placement for Leanne but I had agreed to have her until a place became available in a secure unit. That three months was nearly up and I had been committed and stuck to my side of the bargain.

'So what's going to happen about Julie and Steve?' I asked.

'I've told Becky that I'll meet them for an initial chat although, as I said to her, I'm not promising anything,' Jenny told me.

All I could do was cross my fingers and hope beyond hope that it worked out.

Becky rang me up one afternoon. Leanne had been with me for eleven weeks now so I knew her place at a secure unit was due to come up at any point.

'Jenny and I would like to come round and have a chat with you,' she said.

'Oh God, Leanne's not made another allegation has she?' I asked, my heart sinking.

'No, no, it's nothing to do with that we just want to come and meet with you,' she said.

'OK,' I replied.

It all sounded very official and I concluded the meeting was about moving Leanne to the secure unit and how and when we were going to do that. I felt slightly sick to the stomach that it was actually going to happen. Sometimes, life just isn't fair. When they both arrived, I made us all a cup of tea and we went into the front room to chat.

'So I guess a place has come up for Leanne at a unit,' I said to Jenny.

'Er, no, actually,' she said. 'You know a couple of weeks ago we were talking about Julie and Steve . . .'

I nodded, afraid to allow myself to hope.

'Well I went to meet with them the other week.'

'And what did you think?' I asked nervously.

'I was really impressed,' said Jenny. 'They were enthusiastic and friendly and full of energy. Becky was right, Leanne ticks all their boxes when it comes to the type of child they want to foster.'

Becky and I gave each other a knowing look, as we both knew whose idea it had really been.

'I told them all about Leanne,' continued Jenny. 'I didn't hold back, I was brutally honest and incredibly they still seemed interested. So I spoke to my manager and she's looked at all the information about this couple and we think that Leanne should be placed with them.'

A sense of utter relief and joy filled my body.

'Wow,' I grinned from ear to ear. 'That is absolutely brilliant news.'

I was genuinely delighted.

'So when are you going to tell Leanne?' I asked.

'If it's all right with you I'll pop in after school tonight and give her the news,' said Jenny.

I was so pleased as, in my opinion, this was the best possible outcome for Leanne and I felt she had a real chance to be happy with this couple. They had experience of dealing with problem youngsters. If it didn't work with them then it wasn't going to work with anyone and Social Services would have to look again at a secure unit.

'I know this sounds mad,' I said. 'But if this placement is going to happen please could you ask Julie and Steve to get Leanne a pair of purple roller boots in a size three.'

'OK,' smiled Jenny. 'I'm sure that could be arranged.'

I wanted Leanne's dream about having a mum and a dad and a pair of roller boots to come true.

I was delighted but I was unsure about how Leanne would react. It was another move and yet more upheaval.

Jenny came back after school as she'd promised, sat Leanne down and told her the news. She looked surprised and confused.

'A family?' she questioned. 'But what about the lock-up place? I thought I was going there when I left here.'

'I've watched you here at Maggie's and I've seen how well you have done and how hard you have worked to try and control your behaviour,' said Jenny. 'To be honest we'd always preferred you to be with a family but we hadn't got anybody that would take you, but thanks to Julie and Steve, now we have.'

'Do you know them?' she asked me.

'I've met them,' I said. 'I don't know them very well but they seem really nice and kind.'

'But when will I go?' she asked. 'Can I meet them first?'

I could see her struggling to take all this information in.

'Of course you can meet them,' said Jenny. 'It's Monday today and on Wednesday I'll pick you up from school and we'll pop in to their house for a cup of tea.'

'Does that sound OK?' I asked and Leanne nodded.

Because she was an older child the transfer over to Julie and Steve would probably happen quite quickly within a week. With younger children it tends to be at least two weeks or even longer.

After everyone had left Leanne was very quiet. She sat down at the kitchen table and I poured her a squash while I got on with making dinner.

'That must have been a bit of a surprise,' I said. 'How are you feeling about things?'

'I'm worried,' she said. 'What if they don't like me? What if they get rid of me? Where would I go then?'

'Why wouldn't they like you?' I told her. 'I like you. Louisa likes you. You've been working so hard on your behaviour, Leanne, there's no reason why this shouldn't work and if it doesn't then Jenny will come up with another plan.'

I could see she was confused. I could tell there was a part of her that felt hurt that she was being moved on again.

'If I go and live with them will I still see you?' she asked.

'Of course you will,' I said. 'Julie and Steve are in the same agency as me so I'll see you at all the events and parties.'

'OK,' she said, although she didn't look as though she truly believed me.

Two days later Jenny picked Leanne up after school and they went to Julie and Steve's house for an hour. I was on tenterhooks at home, praying that it had gone OK because I knew this was Leanne's last hope.

'How did it go?' I asked her when she came back, studying her face for any clues. She seemed very quiet and I was worried that it hadn't gone well.

'They seemed nice,' she shrugged.

'Have you told her the best bit?' said Jenny.

'Oh, yeah, they bought me some roller boots,' she smiled. 'And they're purple and the right size.'

'No way,' I grinned, feeling a lot more reassured. 'You always wanted some of those. That's brilliant, Leanne.'

When Leanne had gone up to her room I had a word with Jenny.

'It went OK,' she said. 'Leanne was very quiet and a little bit wary but the roller boots went down well.'

'So what happens next?' I asked.

'They're going to come round to you on Friday for a cup of tea, if that's OK?'

'That's fine,' I said.

On the day I kept it very casual as I didn't want to make it into a big deal. Julie and Steve were as nice as I had remembered them.

'Hello again, Maggie,' smiled Julie. 'We certainly weren't expecting this to happen the last time we saw you.'

Leanne seemed pleased to see them. She rushed downstairs when they arrived and started chatting to them and they were very natural with her. She took them into the kitchen and showed Julie all her cake-decorating paraphernalia while I chatted to Steve.

I wanted to have an honest chat with them before they left. They needed to know that the idea of Leanne skipping off into the sunset with the perfect family was a fantasy. I'd laid the foundations and made her start to accept responsibility for her behaviour but the reality was, there was a long journey ahead.

'I'm so delighted that you want to foster Leanne,' I said. 'I honestly think, as far as foster parents go, you're the perfect match for her.

'However I'm not going to sugarcoat this, because you need to know the truth,' I said. 'There are times when Leanne has been a complete nightmare and she has put me through the mill these past few months. She can be volatile and aggressive, she can be destructive and she has a tendency to fly off the handle.'

'It's OK we know all about Leanne's behaviour,' said Julie. 'Jenny told us everything. In fact it was almost like she was trying to put us off.'

'But it didn't,' laughed Steve.

'She's had so much change and upheaval in her little life so unsurprisingly she doesn't react well to it,' I warned them. 'She's probably going to throw everything at you at first and she'll push you to the limits because it's all strange and new and she's feeling out of control. So my advice to you is try and make sure every rule is in place the minute she walks in the door.'

It was much easier than a few weeks down the line trying to put in rules about things.

'Yes, Becky's chatted to us all about that,' said Julie. 'Did you know she's going to be our link worker as well?'

'That's great news,' I told her.

I was pleased, as that meant there was another way of keeping in contact with them.

Thankfully Julie and Steve didn't seem fazed by anything and I could tell they were itching to welcome Leanne into their home and start their fostering. The thing they seemed most worried about was the fact she was a girl.

'I'm used to two boys,' said Julie. 'I've no idea what young girls like doing.'

'You'll be fine,' I smiled. 'You'll soon work it out and I'm always on the end of the phone if you want to give me a ring.'

That weekend they called in again to collect Leanne's things and the plan was that on Monday, I'd pick her up from school and take her to Julie and Steve's permanently. Although I was prepared for it, I couldn't believe it was happening so fast.

'How are you feeling about Leanne going?' Louisa asked on the Saturday before she left.

'I'm relieved that things have worked out like this,' I said. 'I'm so pleased about where she's going.'

Having to take Leanne to a unit would have caused me and her a lot of upset. This was her best chance and I hoped to the bottom of my heart it would work out.

'Shall we have a little party tomorrow or go out for a meal as it's her last night?' Louisa asked.

When children left we would often mark it in some way.

'I think with Leanne it's best if we keep it as low-key as possible,' I told her.

I didn't want to make a big deal of her leaving as I knew she was feeling nervous and there was the potential that she might kick off and have the mother of all meltdowns.

On her last night I cooked her favourite meal – meatballs and pasta – and afterwards we all sat and watched *Coronation Street* together. I kept it very normal and light but there was a quiet acknowledgement that tomorrow was going to be a fresh start.

Later on I popped my head around Leanne's door to say goodnight. I went and sat on her bed.

'Do you remember our conversation a long time ago when you said you didn't want to go to the secure unit? Remember what you said you wanted?'

She nodded.

'A mum, dad and roller boots.'

'Well you've got it now, so it's up to you what you do with it. I think Julie and Steve are great and this is a big chance for you to move forward with your life. Louisa and I are really fond of you and we're going to miss you but this is the best

222

thing that I could have hoped for.' I smiled. 'I want you to go and be happy.'

'I'll try.' She smiled back.

In the morning she said goodbye to Louisa.

'I hope you're really happy in your new home,' Louisa told her. 'Julie and Steve seem lovely. And make sure you behave,' she teased.

'I will,' grinned Leanne. 'I'm not as cross as I used to be any more.'

I smiled as I watched the two of them chatting. Leanne was right. A comment like that, even a few weeks ago, would probably have sent her flying off the handle. Thankfully now she was a calmer and, dare I say it, happier little girl.

'We're going to miss you,' Louisa told her. 'The house is going to be very quiet without you.'

Leanne grinned and gave her a hug.

'See you soon,' she said. 'I might see you at the agency Christmas party?'

'Yeah, I'm sure you will,' Louisa told her. 'Maggie normally drags me along to that.'

The pair of them hadn't got off to the best of starts but it was lovely to see the bond that had developed between them. Louisa was part of my family and I knew she got attached to children, no matter what their problems, just like I did. It was always a big change for us when they moved on.

'I'll pack the rest of your stuff in the car and see you after school,' I told her.

When I went to collect Leanne later that afternoon, she was silent on the fifteen-minute journey to Julie and Steve's house. She was as quiet as a mouse.

We pulled up outside and just before she got out of the car, she turned to me.

'I will miss you, Maggie,' she said.

'I'll miss you too, sweetheart,' I told her.

She jumped out of the car while I took a minute to swallow the lump in my throat. That was such a huge statement from a child who had never attached to anyone for long and who pushed everyone away with her behaviour. A child who had had thirty homes in her short life.

I took a deep breath and composed myself as I walked over to Julie and Steve.

'All set?' I asked and they nodded excitedly.

'I'm going to make this very quick and not prolong it,' I said. 'I'm not one for long goodbyes.'

I gave Leanne a hug.

'Bye, lovey,' I said, breathing in the smell of her hair. 'And I have no doubt that I'll see you very soon.'

'Bye,' she said and I felt her arms cling tightly on to me.

Afterwards I got into the car and gave them a cheery wave as I drove away. As soon as they were out of sight, I couldn't hold back any more.

By the time I pulled up outside my friend Vicky's house, my face was streaked with tears.

'Oh, Maggie,' she sighed when she saw me. 'Have you not learnt to wear waterproof mascara on the days you say bye to kids.'

I smiled.

'They're good tears really,' I said.

My heart was heavy that another child had gone but I was happy for Leanne.

'You look like you could do with a cuddle,' Vicky smiled, plonking the six-month-old baby boy she was fostering into my arms.

Feeling the warmth of a chubby little baby was really comforting and I snuggled into him.

'So how are you, Maggie?' Vicky asked.

'Numb,' I said. 'Heavy-hearted. Pleased. Absolutely exhausted.'

'Wow,' she laughed. 'Well you should be really proud of yourself. You did the best you could for her in such a short space of time.'

'I tried,' I said.

At least I'd managed to give Leanne – the girl that no one wanted – another chance with a family and that's all I could have wished for her.

Fostering Leanne had taught me that it was never too late. However terribly a child behaved, no matter how many moves they'd had, it was never too late to try and find them a stable, happy home. There was always hope.

Epilogue

A few months after Leanne had left I met Julie at a training day.

'How's it going?' I asked her.

'I'm exhausted, Maggie,' she said. 'You were right. She's pushed us and tested us to the limits but we're surviving.'

'It's completely different 24/7 isn't it?' I said.

'It certainly is,' she smiled. 'But you know what, Maggie, we love her, we really do.'

I was so pleased to hear that. As time went on I kept in touch with Julie and Steve. Becky updated me how they were doing and I saw them at agency events.

I know they had some hard times with Leanne and it wasn't easy. I occasionally did respite care for them and took Leanne for the odd weekend so they could have a break.

Leanne is eighteen now and she still lives with Julie and Steve. She will always be volatile and have the occasional outburst but Julie and Steve have given her the stability and the continuity of care that she'd never had before, and with them she has thrived. I couldn't be more proud of how far she's come.

I, on the other hand, got my mother and baby placement, but that's a whole other story . . .

Acknowledgements

Thank you to my children, Tess, Pete and Sam, who are such a big part of my fostering today however I had not met you when Ben, Damien, Noah, Edward, Leanne and Louise came into my home. To my wide circle of fostering friends – you know who you are! Your support and your laughter are valued. To my friend Andrew B for your continued encouragement and care. Thanks also to Heather Bishop who spent many hours listening and enabled this story to be told, my literary agent Rowan Lawton and to Anna Valentine and the team at Trapeze for giving me the opportunity to share these stories.

A Note from Maggie

I really hope you enjoyed reading about Ben, Damien, Noah, Edward and Leanne's stories. I love sharing my experiences of fostering with you, and I also love hearing what you think about them. If you enjoyed this book, or any of my others, please think about leaving a review online. I know other readers really benefit from your thoughts, and I do too.

To be the first to hear about my new books, you can keep in touch on my Facebook page @MaggieHartleyAuthor. I find it inspiring to learn about your own experiences of fostering and adoption, and to read your comments and reviews.

Finally, thank you so much for choosing to read *Too Scared to Cry*. If you enjoyed it, there are others available including *Tiny Prisoners*, *The Little Ghost Girl*, *Too Young to be a Mum*, *Who Will Love Me Now*, *Battered, Broken, Healed*, *Sold to be a Wife* and *Is It My Fault Mummy?*. I hope you'll enjoy my next story just as much.

Maggie Hartley

EXCLUSIVE SAMPLE CHAPTER FROM

Who Will Love Me Now?

ONE

On the Cards

The woman carefully shuffled the pack of cards and fanned them out, face down, in front of me.

'Pick seven,' she told me.

After I'd done as she'd asked, she put the cards I'd chosen back down on the table and turned them over one by one.

She smiled.

'What is it?' I asked. 'What can you see?'

'Ooh, lots of things,' she said. 'What would you like to ask me, my dear?'

To be honest, I wasn't sure, as I'd never done this before. My friend Vicky, who was also a foster carer, had convinced me that having a tarot card reading at home one morning would be a bit of fun.

'Marjorie's meant to be really good,' she'd told me. 'My sister-in-law swears by her. She sees her every six months.'

I thought it was all mumbo jumbo but she'd persuaded me and so here we were. Vicky was in the kitchen, waiting to have her reading after mine. I don't know what I was expecting but

Marjorie was an ordinary-looking lady in her fifties. It was hard to believe that this woman in jeans, a jumper and fake UGG boots could predict my future, but I was willing to give it a go.

'I've got a question for you,' I said. 'When will I be getting more children to foster?'

Marjorie picked up the first card, which had a picture of a king holding a gold disc on it.

'Ah, this suit of the tarot cards is all about your work and I can see that you love what you do very much,' she said. 'In fact, it's more of a vocation than a job for you. The good news is the cards are telling me that a new child will be arriving soon.'

'Ooh, how soon?' I asked.

'The cards are saying that there's a child on the way to you as we speak.'

'Really?' I gasped. 'Right now?'

Marjorie nodded.

'Is it a girl or a boy?' I asked. 'How old are they?'

'That, I'm afraid, I don't know,' she said. 'But if the cards are right then it won't be long before you find out.'

There were no other surprise revelations in the rest of my reading but I was excited at the possibility that I might be getting a new foster placement.

'What did she say?' Vicky asked when I went to get her from the kitchen for her reading.

'Well, I'm not going to win the lottery or meet the man of my dreams, but apparently there's a new foster placement on its way to me right now.'

'That's brilliant news,' she said.

I'd been on the available list with my fostering agency for the past couple of weeks but, so far, nothing had come up.

'I hope she's right,' I told Vicky. 'I'm ready for a new challenge.'

At that time I had two children living with me. Louisa had been with me since her parents had been tragically killed in a car crash five years ago. Alone and struggling to cope with her grief, she'd been painfully shy at first but she had turned into a strong, confident, determined young woman who I was very proud of. She'd recently turned eighteen so she was now an adult and officially out of the care system. Even though I wasn't legally fostering her any more, she would always be part of my family and she knew she could live with me for as long as she wanted to. She had finished a course in childcare and had just got a job as a nanny for a local family, which she was really enjoying.

Then there was baby Ryan who was upstairs having his morning nap. He was six months old now and had been with me since he was two weeks old when his teenage parents had taken him to hospital, saying that he'd rolled off the sofa and bumped his head. Staff had been suspicious of this explanation as a baby that young doesn't roll and X-rays had shown he'd also got a fractured rib. An emergency protection order had been issued and he'd immediately been taken into care. The Crown Prosecution Service was still looking into whether there was enough evidence to charge his parents with hurting him. The plan was that Ryan would eventually go for adoption and I was looking after him until then. I had leapt at the chance to care for Ryan. It was heartbreaking to think that a tiny baby had gone through such pain and cruelty at the hands of the two people who were supposed to love him the most. It wasn't hard to get attached to babies and Ryan was a lovely smiley little boy. He had a lovely thick mop of blond curls and bright blue eyes that made him look like a little cherub. Thankfully, so far he didn't seem to have been affected by the traumatic start that he'd had to his life.

You might think that I had my hands full with a teenager and a young baby to look after, but the truth was, life was a bit too quiet for me. Louisa was at work all day or out with her friends and Ryan was an easy baby. I liked the noise and the chaos of having several children living with me and I had plenty of room in my six-bed house. My other long-term foster placement, Lily, had gone back to live with her birth mother several months ago and I'd said goodbye to teenage mum Jess and her baby Jimmy around the same time, as they now had their own place along with Jimmy's dad Darren. Since they'd all left I'd had a few respite placements but now I was hoping for something a bit more long term.

Although I always liked the challenge of stroppy teenagers, my ideal was a child or children under twelve. I found that age group particularly interesting – I liked the endless questions, the funny things they said and the way their minds were like little sponges soaking up everything around them.

Yep, life is a bit too quiet and organised for me at the minute, I thought as I flicked the kettle on to make everyone a cup of tea.

I was putting some digestive biscuits onto a plate when my mobile rang. I recognised the number flashing up on the screen – it was Becky my supervising social worker from the fostering agency I worked for. She'd been my link worker ever since I'd joined the agency well over a year ago and we got on really well.

'Hi, Maggie,' she said. 'I'm not disturbing anything, am I?'

'If I told you what was going on at my house at the minute you'd think I was mad.' I smiled, thinking about the tarot card reader in the front room. 'What can I do for you?'

'I've just had a call from a social worker called Kate Lewis who said she'd worked with you in the past.'

She was at the local authority that I'd worked for before I'd moved to the agency. She'd been the social worker on a couple of placements I'd had way back when I'd first started fostering. I remembered Kate because she was very well spoken and was always perfectly turned out with swishy hair and expensive-looking clothes.

The cases we'd worked on together had been two troubled teens – one of them had threatened me with a gun and the other was a persistent runaway so they had both been a challenge, to say the least.

'Gosh that was years ago,' I told Becky. 'I'm surprised she remembers me.'

'Well, you must have made an impression as she asked for you specifically,' she replied. 'She needs someone to take an emergency placement and she said you were good with tricky cases.'

'Ah, it's one of those, is it?' I asked, wondering exactly what 'tricky' meant in this situation. 'Have you got any more details about the child or how long they're likely to be with me?'

'All I know is that it's a ten-year-old girl and Kate needs an answer ASAP as she has to be placed today.'

Sometimes in fostering, especially when it's an emergency placement, you have to make a decision based on only the scantiest of information.

'OK,' I said. 'Tell Kate I'll take her.'

I'd been hoping for a child under twelve and because Kate had asked for me personally I felt obliged to help.

'Either Kate or I will be in touch when we know more about when she'll be arriving,' she said.

'No problem,' I said. 'Speak soon.'

As I hung up, Vicky came into the kitchen with Marjorie the tarot card reader.

'You won't believe this, but that was my link worker from the fostering agency offering me a new placement,' I told them. 'It's a little girl. She's coming today.'

'You see,' said Marjorie. 'The cards are never wrong.'

She left with a big smile on her face, clearly delighted that one of her predictions had come true. Ryan was still asleep so Vicky stuck around for a cup of tea and a chat.

'Do you need a hand getting the bedroom ready?' she asked me.

'I don't think there's much to do,' I said. 'I'll probably put her in Lily's old room.'

I'd recently done a respite placement for a weekend for three siblings so there were bunk beds in there now, as well as a single bed.

'Do you think I should take the bunks down?' I asked Vicky. 'There's more room in there when it's just a single.'

'I'd leave it until you know a bit more about her,' she said.

She was right. For all I knew, the girl might only be with me for a few days, depending on the circumstances.

'I'll be off now, so you can get ready for your new arrival,' said Vicky. 'As the cards predicted.'

'A coincidence, if you ask me.' I smiled. 'I'm still not sure I believe in all that and, besides, it's not exactly a surprise when I've been on the vacant list for weeks.'

When Vicky had gone, I woke Ryan up from his nap and began making his lunch. He was such a happy boy and even though I'd disturbed him from a deep sleep, he grinned up at me with his big blue eyes. Ryan was used to having all my attention when Louisa was at work and I hoped the little girl who was on her way to us liked babies and would grow to love him as much as I did. He'd recently started on solids so I was busy mashing some carrot and swede up for him when my phone went.

'Hi, Kate, it's nice to hear from you after all these years,' I said, recognising the well-spoken voice on the other end of the line. 'My link worker Becky said you'd be calling.'

'Yes,' she said. 'I've got a case I thought you might be able to help with. It's a ten-year-old girl called Kirsty.'

'Becky said it was an emergency placement so I'm assuming she's about to be taken into care today?' I asked.

'Actually, she's already in care,' Kate explained. 'She's been fostered long term by the same couple since she was a toddler.'

'Oh, I see,' I said, surprised.

This case was getting more intriguing, and confusing, by the minute.

'I haven't got huge amounts of time to fill you in now but the gist of it is that Kirsty's lived with Pat and Mike since she was nine months old.

'This morning she was at home with Pat when she collapsed. Kirsty rang Social Services as she wasn't sure what to do and found the number on Pat's phone.

'One of my colleagues phoned an ambulance and Pat was rushed to hospital.'

'Oh no,' I said. 'That's terrible. How is she?'

'All I know is that the doctors think it was a heart attack and Mike is up at the hospital with her now.

'They're obviously both very shocked so we need someone to look after Kirsty until we know what Pat's prognosis is and what's happening.'

'The poor girl,' I said.

It must have been terrifying for her to see her foster mother keel over like that in front of her and then be rushed off in an ambulance.

While Kate was explaining all this to me, I could hear someone shouting and carrying on in the background.

'Who on earth's that?' I asked.

'That's Kirsty,' she told me. 'She's a bit – how can I put this? – lively.

'Would you mind having a quick word with her, Maggie? She's insisting that she talks to you.'

'I wanna speak to her,' I heard a voice say. 'Gimme the phone.'

'Here you go,' I heard Kate say.

'Hello, is that Kirsty?' I asked. 'I'm Maggie. I hear you're coming to stay with me while your foster mum's in hospital.'

'Yeah,' she said. 'Have you got any pets? I love animals, especially dogs, which I love more than cats.

'Will I have my own bedroom? I hope so. And will there be lots of toys for me to play with? I love toys.'

She hardly paused for breath as she fired off one question after another without giving me the time to answer. She certainly wasn't the traumatised, scared little girl that I had expected. She sounded excited, like she was going on a holiday or a big adventure.

'I've got two cats called Billy and Mog,' I told her when I finally managed to get a word in edgeways.

'Oh,' she said. 'Well, I suppose I'll get used to them. I like rabbits too. Have you got any rabbits? I also like hamsters and gerbils but not mice. Don't like their tails.'

'Kirsty, please give me the phone back now. I need to speak to Maggie,' I heard Kate say.

She must have managed to grab her mobile off her as she finally came back on the line.

'Hi, Maggie. Sorry about that,' she said.

'Well that was, erm, interesting,' I said. 'She certainly sounds lively. Isn't she at all upset by what happened today?'

'Apparently not,' sighed Kate.

It was all very odd. However, I'd been doing this job long enough to know that trauma and shock could manifest themselves in lots of different ways. Kids often reacted entirely differently from how you expected them to.

Kate explained that she was helping Kirsty to get some of her things together.

'She's not being that helpful at the minute,' she told me quietly. 'But hopefully we'll be with you in an hour or so.'

'That's no problem,' I said. 'I'm in for the rest of the day so turn up whenever. I'm sure Becky gave you my address.'

In fact, it was a whole three hours later when the doorbell rang at just after 4 p.m. I picked up Ryan and went to answer it.

It was a freezing cold January day so it was already dark outside as I opened the door. On the doorstep was an extremely harassed-looking Kate. She was exactly as I'd remembered her – albeit slightly older and a bit more dishevelled. Standing next to her was a chubby little girl with long light brown wavy hair, dressed in leggings and a jumper, with a smug look on her face.

'Sorry we're late,' said Kate, giving me a weary smile. 'Things took slightly longer than I was anticipating.'

'No problem,' I told her.

'And you must be Kirsty,' I said, turning to the little girl. 'It's nice to meet you.'

She grinned at me.

'Oh, you've got a baby!' she yelled as she saw Ryan wriggling around in my arms. 'I love babies. Can I hold him?'

I hung onto him for dear life as she tried to grab him from me.

'That's probably not a good idea, lovey,' I told her gently. 'He's a lot heavier than he looks. Why don't you come in and let him get used to you first and then perhaps you can have a cuddle later on.

'Would you like a drink or anything to eat?' I asked as they came into the hallway.

'No thanks,' said Kirsty. 'Kate bought me an ice cream on the way here.'

'An ice cream?' I questioned, surprised.

It was a chilly winter's day, not exactly traditional ice cream weather.

'I had to stop and get her one,' Kate muttered, rolling her eyes. 'It was the only way I could persuade her to get in the car with me.'

I could tell that Kate had had a long, exhausting battle getting this child to my house. Kirsty, meanwhile, seemed full of energy and was as chirpy as she had been when I'd spoken to her on the phone earlier.

'Where's my room?' she asked. 'Can I see my room? I hope it's not pink. I hate pink. I can't sleep in a pink room. Are there any toys up there? I didn't bring any with me.'

It really was quite bizarre. I would have expected that a child her age who had seen their parent collapse in front of them before being taken to stay with a stranger would be weepy or anxious, or at least a little bit quiet and subdued. Kirsty, however, seemed full of life and entirely unaffected by the day's traumatic events.

'I need to have a quick word with Kate in the kitchen so I'll put the TV on and you can watch a cartoon while we have a chat,' I told her. 'I'll show you your bedroom later.'

'I don't like cartoons,' she scowled.

'Well, you can find something you do like for ten minutes,' I said, handing her the remote.

Kate and I walked through to the kitchen.

'She seems full of energy,' I said, putting Ryan down in his playpen.

'Yes, she certainly is,' sighed Kate.

'I'm afraid I've got to rush off somewhere now,' she added. 'So tell me, what do you need to know?'

She had put me a bit on the spot.

'Oh, er, OK,' I said. 'Is she on any medication and what do I need to do about school?'

It was Thursday so I was assuming that she'd be going the following day.

'She's not on any medication and don't worry about school,' said Kate. 'After everything that's happened, she can have the day off tomorrow. I've already rung the school and told them.

'Coincidentally they've got an inset day on Monday and anyway she'll probably be back home by then.'

By the sounds of it, this was going to be another short respite placement.

'By the way, Kirsty's been with Mike and Pat for so long she calls them Mum and Dad,' she told me.

'That's fine,' I said. 'Have you heard any more about how her mum is?'

'When I leave here I'm going to give Mike a call so I'll let you know if there are any updates,' she said.

'Before I go, shall we quickly take Kirsty up to her bedroom so I can check it?' asked Kate. 'I'm sorry, but you know it's procedure now.'

'Of course,' I said.

Guidance had recently been brought in that said whenever a foster parent took on a new child, the child's social worker had to check where they would be sleeping. This was because there had been reports about a couple of foster carers who, desperate to get more money, had squashed several children into one room with just mattresses on the floor rather than proper beds.

I picked up Ryan and we went to get Kirsty from the front room.

'Maggie's going to show us where you're going to be sleeping,' Kate told her.

'Yippee!' She smiled, jumping up.

We all trooped upstairs to the bedroom and Kirsty looked around.

'This is a lovely room, isn't it, Kirsty?' said Kate. 'I'm sure you'll be very comfy here for the next few days.'

'It's OK,' she huffed. 'But I don't like the pink blanket. Remember, Maggie, I told you I didn't like pink? I'd be OK with a blue one or a red one cos I like red too. Or yellow. Just not pink, cos it makes me feel sick.'

This child certainly liked to talk.

'That's not a problem,' I told her. 'I can get you another blanket.'

'Look at all these beds,' she sighed. 'Which one shall I sleep in? I like the bottom bunk, but I like the top bunk too cos you can see everything from up high, but then I might fall out and hurt myself.'

'Right, well, I'd better be going,' said Kate, interrupting Kirsty's monologue.

'I'll come down with you and see you out then I can bring Kirsty's stuff up,' I said, wanting a few minutes alone with Kate.

'She likes to talk,' I said to Kate as I opened the front door.

'Yes, it's incessant,' she said. 'I think it's when she's anxious or nervous and I suppose it's not surprising after what happened today.'

I really felt for Kirsty.

'Keep me updated if you hear anything from the hospital,' I told her.

'I will,' she said. 'I'll give Kirsty a call tomorrow.'

After Kate had gone, I went back upstairs with the small holdall that she had brought containing Kirsty's pyjamas and a couple of changes of clothes.

I sat down on the bed with Ryan on my knee.

'How are you feeling, Kirsty?' I asked. 'You've had a long day. It must have been so scary for you when your mum collapsed.'

'She'll be OK.' She shrugged. 'Kate said the doctors will make her better.

'Can I have some tea now?' She smiled. 'I'm hungry.'

She didn't quite seem to grasp the seriousness of what had happened. All I could hope was that Kate was right and Kirsty's foster mum was going to pull through, because it was going to be one heck of a shock for this little girl if she didn't.

TINY PRISONERS

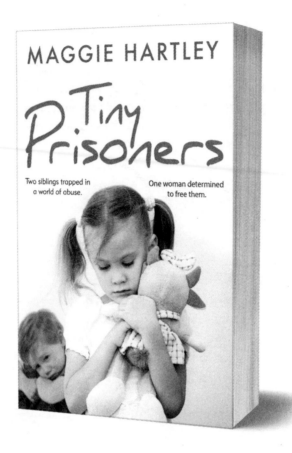

Evie and Elliot are scrawny, filthy and wide-eyed with fear when they turn up on foster carer Maggie Hartley's doorstep. They're too afraid to leave the house and any intrusion of the outside world sends them into a panic. It's up to Maggie to unlock the truth of their heart-breaking upbringing, and to help them learn to smile again.

THE LITTLE GHOST GIRL

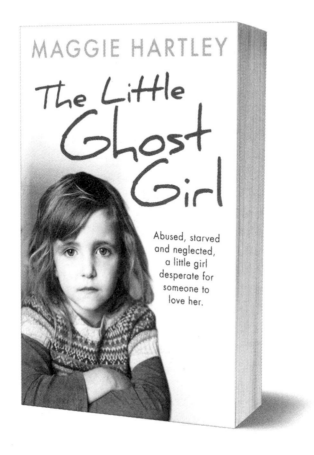

Ruth is a ghost of a girl when she arrives into foster mother Maggie Hartley's care. Pale, frail and withdrawn, it's clear to Maggie that Ruth had seen and experienced things that no 11-year-old should have to. Ruth is in desperate need of help, but can Maggie get through to her and unearth the harrowing secret she carries?

TOO YOUNG TO BE A MUM

Too Young to be a Mum

Can Jess learn to be a good mummy, when she is only a child herself?

MAGGIE HARTLEY

When sixteen-year-old Jess arrives on foster carer Maggie Hartley's doorstep with her newborn son Jimmy, she has nowhere else to go. With social services threatening to take baby Jimmy into care, Jess knows that Maggie is her only chance of keeping her son. Can Maggie help Jess learn to become a mum?

WHO WILL LOVE ME NOW?

When ten-year-old Kirsty arrives at the home of foster carer Maggie Hartley, she is reeling from the rejection of her long-term foster family. She acts out, smashing up Maggie's home. But when she threatens to hurt the baby boy Maggie has fostered since birth, Maggie is placed in an impossible position; one that calls in to question her decision to become a foster carer in the first place...

BATTERED, BROKEN, HEALED

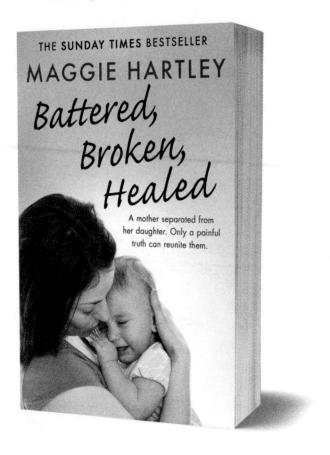

Six-week-old baby Jasmine comes to stay with Maggie after she is removed from her home. Neighbours have repeatedly called the police on suspicion of domestic violence, but her timid mother Hailey vehemently denies that anything is wrong. Can Maggie persuade Hailey to admit what's going on behind closed doors so that mother and baby can be reunited?

SOLD TO BE A WIFE

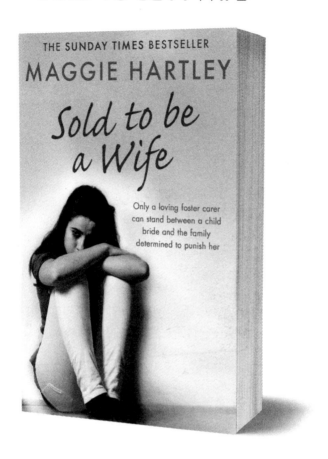

THE SUNDAY TIMES BESTSELLER
MAGGIE HARTLEY
Sold to be a Wife

Only a loving foster carer
can stand between a child
bride and the family
determined to punish her

Fourteen-year-old Shazia has been taken into care over a
fears that her family are planning to send her to Pakistan
for an arranged marriage. But with Shazia denying
everything and with social services unable to find any
evidence, Shazia is eventually allowed to return home. But
when Maggie wakes up a few weeks later in the middle of
the night to a call from the terrified Shazia, it looks like her
worst fears have been confirmed...

DENIED A MUMMY

THE SUNDAY TIMES BESTSELLER

MAGGIE HARTLEY

Denied a Mummy

The heartbreaking story of three little children searching for someone to love them

Maggie has her work cut out for her when her latest placement arrives on her doorstep; two little boys, aged five and seven and their eight-year-old sister. Having suffered extensive abuse and neglect, Maggie must slowly work through their trauma with love and care. But when a couple is approved to adopt the siblings, alarm bells start to ring. Maggie tries to put her own fears to one side but she can't shake the feeling of dread as she waves goodbye to them. Will these vulnerable children ever find a forever family?

TOO SCARED TO CRY

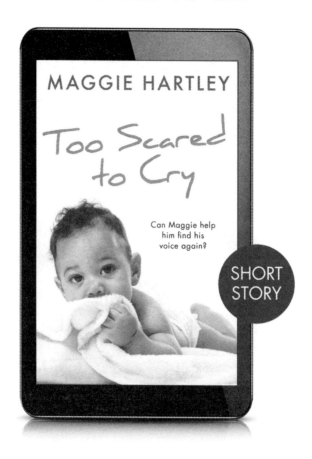

MAGGIE HARTLEY

Too Scared to Cry

Can Maggie help
him find his
voice again?

SHORT
STORY

A baby too scared to cry. Two toddlers too scared to
speak. This is the dramatic short story of three traumatised
siblings, whose lives are transformed by the love of foster
carer Maggie Hartley.

IS IT MY FAULT MUMMY?

Seven-year-old Paris is trapped in a prison of guilt.
Devastated after the death of her baby brother, Joel,
Maggie faces one of the most heartbreaking cases yet as
she tries to break down the wall of guilt surrounding this
damaged little girl.

A FAMILY FOR CHRISTMAS

A tragic accident leaves the life of toddler Edward
changed forever and his family wracked with guilt.
Will Maggie be able to help this family grieve for the son
they've lost and learn to love the little boy he is now?
And will Edward have a family to go home to
at Christmas?

THE GIRL NO ONE WANTED

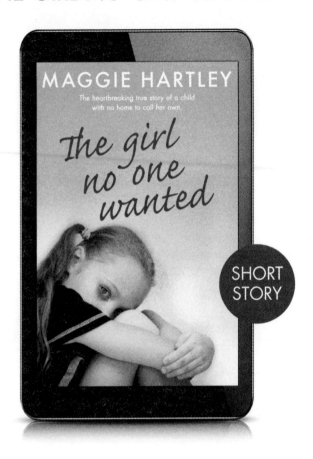

MAGGIE HARTLEY

The heartbreaking true story of a child with no home to call her own.

the girl no one wanted

SHORT STORY

Eleven-year-old Leanne is out of control. With over forty placements in her short life, no local foster carers are willing to take in this angry and damaged little girl. Maggie is Leanne's only hope, and her last chance. If this placement fails, Leanne will have to be put in a secure unit. Where most others would simply walk away, Maggie refuses to give up on the little girl who's never known love.